AF256378

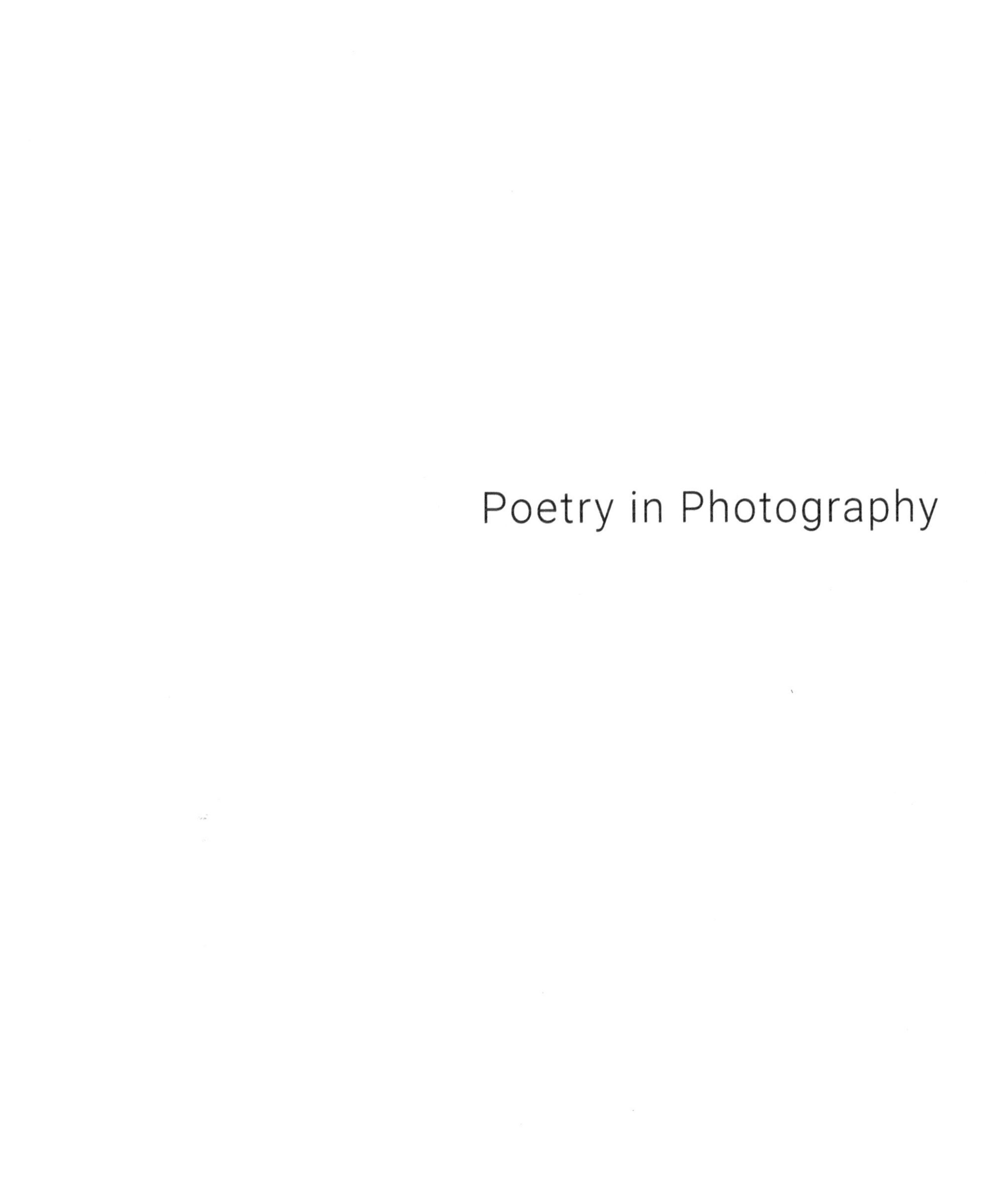

Poetry in Photography

Poetry in Photography

A Journey of a Wandering Teacher

Vincent Nugroho

Copyright © 2023 by Vincent Nugroho
All rights reserved. No part of this book may be reproduced in any form without written permission from the author or publisher.

Poems by Vincent Nugroho
Photos by Vincent Nugroho

Library and Archives Canada Cataloging in Publication

Nugroho, Vincent
Poetry in Photography: A Journey of a Wandering Teacher

ISBN 978-1-7388674-0-0

Published by Vincent Nugroho
Cover Design by Vincent Nugroho

CONTENTS

CONTENTS

CONTENTS

CONTENTS

CONTENTS

CONTENTS

CONTENTS

CONTENTS

CONTENTS

In the vast realm of creative pursuits, from crafting flashcards for eager students to designing whimsical kites that awaken the child within me, I have discovered a profound truth: the process of creation is not only enjoyable but often meditative. In the midst of artistic endeavors, I have found myself lost in a delightful flow, occasionally taking a break for a sip of coffee, only to return with renewed vigor.

Witnessing the fruits of my labor and knowing that my creations serve a meaningful purpose brings both delight and profound gratification. Yet, beyond the joy of composing content, there is another passion that stirs my soul - the art of capturing moments through photography. Each click of the camera feels like crafting a story of endless bliss, so engrossed that I sometimes forget meals or thirst while under the spell of storytelling images. Each angle, every possible variation in composition, consumes me in a rhythm of gleeful immersion.

Upon reflection, I've come to realize that my photographs often embody a simplistic perspective. Embracing this sense of naivety proved to be liberating and inspiring. It compelled me to dig deeper into my approach, embracing the purity that minimalism offers, and refusing to let go.

The realization of seeing things with newfound clarity may have emerged from my encounter with the Japanese haiku and the Irish limerick. Each carrying its own essence - one profound, the other lighthearted - I found admiration in both. The idea of blending the playful rhythm of rhyming limericks with the elegant simplicity of haiku began to take root, igniting a creative itch that demanded satisfaction. And so, I envisioned a unique fusion, like the harmonious union of two artistic souls.

In this book, I embark on a journey to tell a simple yet joyous story, drawing inspiration from the structure of haiku while cherishing the freedom to have fun. The result, I hope, will resonate with both you and me, taking us on an imaginative adventure of words and images.

I owe my heartfelt gratitude to the Halifax Central Library for providing the perfect sanctuary, offering its enriching facilities and abundant resources. It is here that the seeds of this endeavor found fertile ground, and I hope that what has blossomed here will bring understanding and joy to all who explore its pages. May this collection be a celebration of creativity, an homage to simplicity, and a union of diverse artistic expressions.

With eager anticipation, I invite you to immerse yourself in the fusion of haiku and limericks, where creativity knows no bounds, and the joy of making finds its fullest expression.

Welcome to the delightful union of two poetic worlds.

Halifax Public Libraries
Halifax, Nova Scotia,
Canada

For the facilities and resources needed to put my story into

Poetry in Photography: A Journey of a Wandering Teacher

I want to dedicate this book to

Afa

Gary and Nancy

A Day in the Life

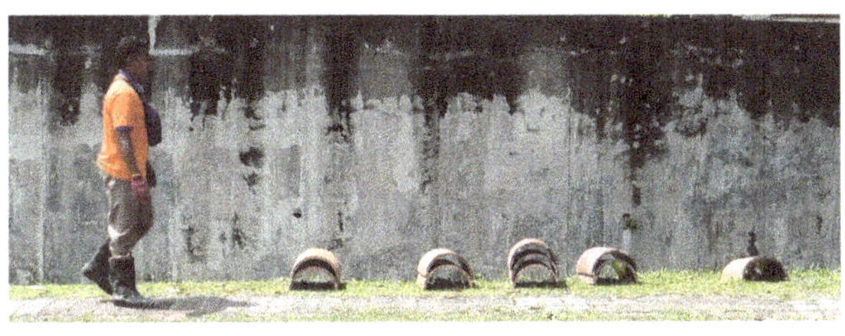

Hurdles in the way
Some can make or break your day
Wisdom what you say

Photo taken in 2019

Location: Penang, Malaysia

The clay drainage pipes on the ground did not look significant when I was walking the sidewalk where the man was,

but the way they were laid out somehow "told" me to cross the street to have a different look.

I was rewarded for "listening".

The man, who happened to be walking toward them,

the approach toward what lies ahead,

inspired a tale to tell of a timeline.

Abstract Sculptor

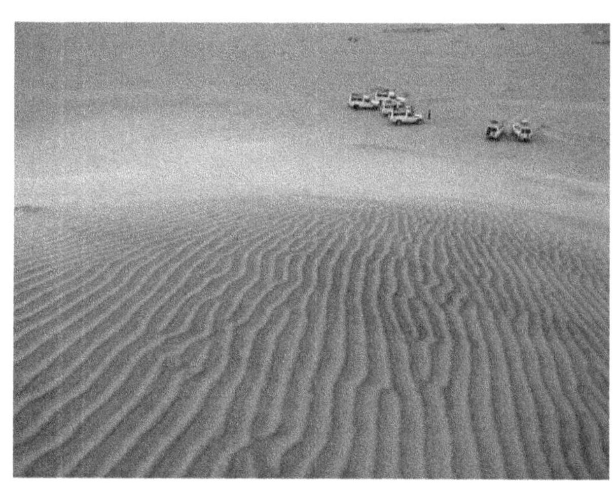

Carving surfaces
Leaving sculptured rock faces
Footprints on the waves

Photo taken in 2016

Location: Sahara Desert, Egypt

Despite the scorching heat during the day, desert sand at dawn is soothing cool.

The sky was lit low on one side, revealing the texture in the foreground up this dune;

which may otherwise look quite different by noon.

An Uplift

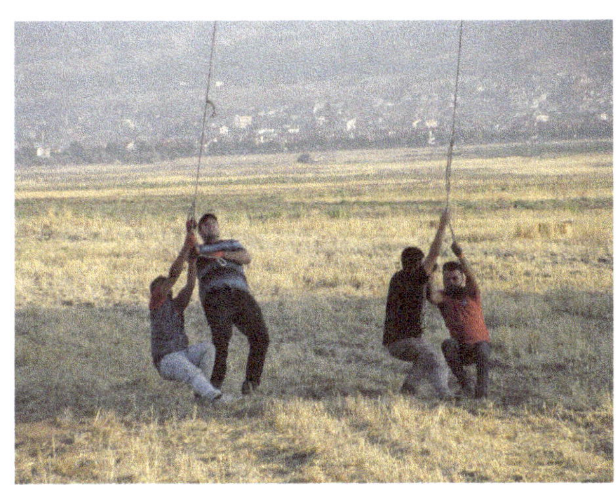

Nice view from the peak
What you have become shall speak
In reaching the peak

Photo taken in 2018

Location: Cappadocia, Turkey

Hot air balloons rise as hot air is lighter than cool air.

Upon landing, the hot air is still trapped inside the envelope (the balloon)

until it cools down before the balloon collapses.

Or you can pull it down when it's hot; instead of waiting.

Ancient Scholar

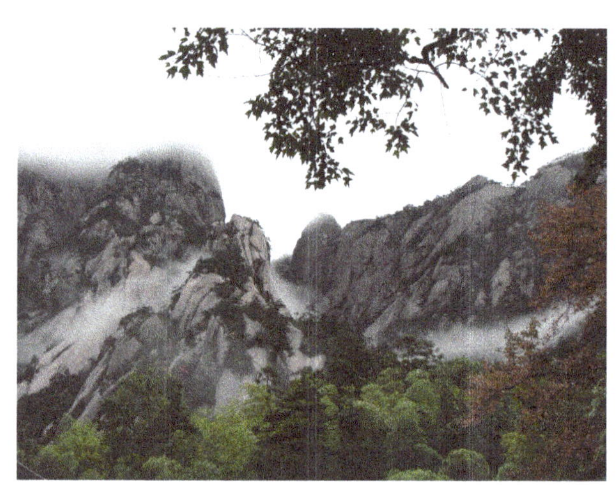

He plucks the zither
Chess player and brush painter
Fine calligrapher

(Inspired by the four traits required of an ancient Chinese scholar)

Photo taken in 2008

Location: Huangshan, China

As I was writing about this photo, I came across this resembling painting:

<https://www.comuseum.com/painting/masters/huang-gongwang/dwelling-in-the-fuchun-mountains/>

Around the Corner

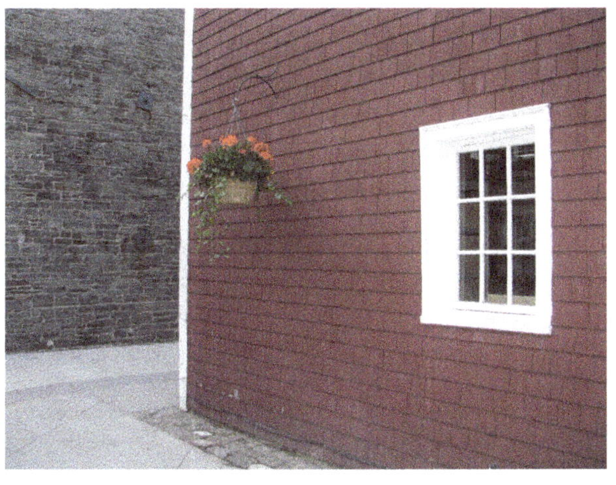

Around the corner
A question mark to ponder
What's there I wonder

Photo taken in 2008

Location: Halifax, Canada

This is one of Halifax's many historical buildings.

I like the mysterious feel this place conjures,

one can hear footsteps from around the corner.

For more information about Nova Scotia's heritage buildings:

<https://cch.novascotia.ca/exploring-our-past/heritage-property>

Attachment

To pray on cliff face
There is some gripping to ace
And path up to trace

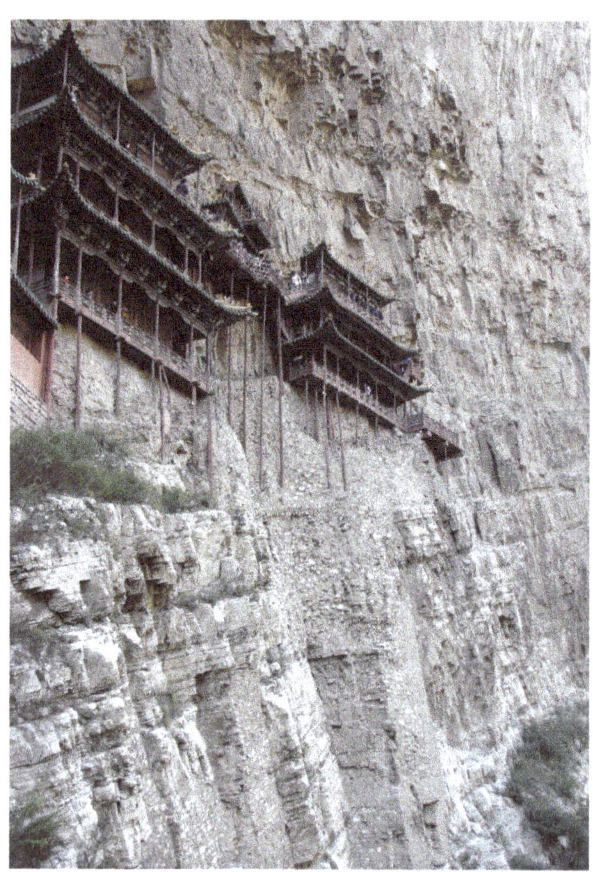

Photo taken in 2008

Location: Xuankongsi, China

The first time I saw it was in a photo. It gave me the impression that it was glued to the steep cliff wall. I told myself, I must see it in person. There was no direct transport to here, the bus driver told me to get off to take the taxi already waiting and that the taxi fare was already included in the bus ticket. I complied, gleefully. The taxi waited on the way back for a fix fare. My architecture bug was satisfied to have seen it in person.

Backlit

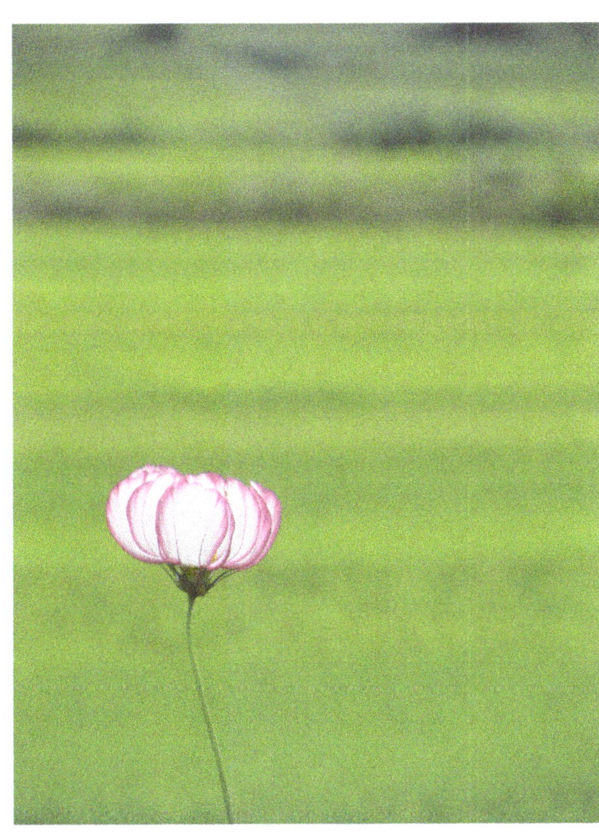

Pierced by late sun ray
Skeleton is on display
On this summer day

Photo taken in 2018

Location: Somewhere in Yunnan, China

The breeze was pleasant, but hard for this beauty to stay still, especially on such a long slim stem. Took me several attempts to capture the moment. Such result is possible when the sun (not in the frame) is behind the flower, lighting it from the back side.

Baking Record

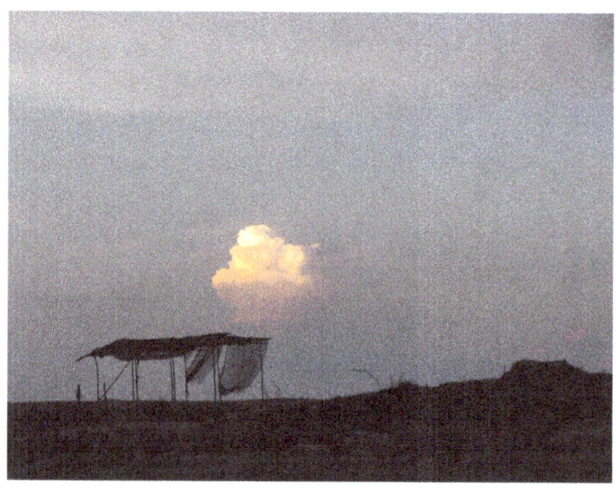

Puff goes my oven
Good old smoke goes to heaven
Ceiling dough flattened

Photo taken in 2010

Location: Chongkhneas, Cambodia

It was dry season, my boat was on shallow water,

low enough to enhance this drama: A "flame" hovering low.

The breeze adds life to the flowing curtains in the dark foreground.

One can tell from the cloud, the sun has partially set into the horizon,

only the tip of the sun meeting the tip of the cloud; and this moment is brief.

Beach Development

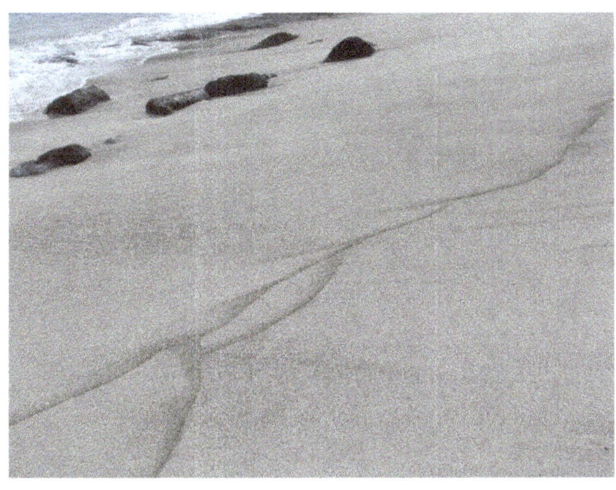

As the waves escape
So is the sand of this cape
From claiming a stake

Photo taken in 2017

Location: Nusa Lembongan, Indonesia

Will it someday be "developed"?

Beauty in the Rain

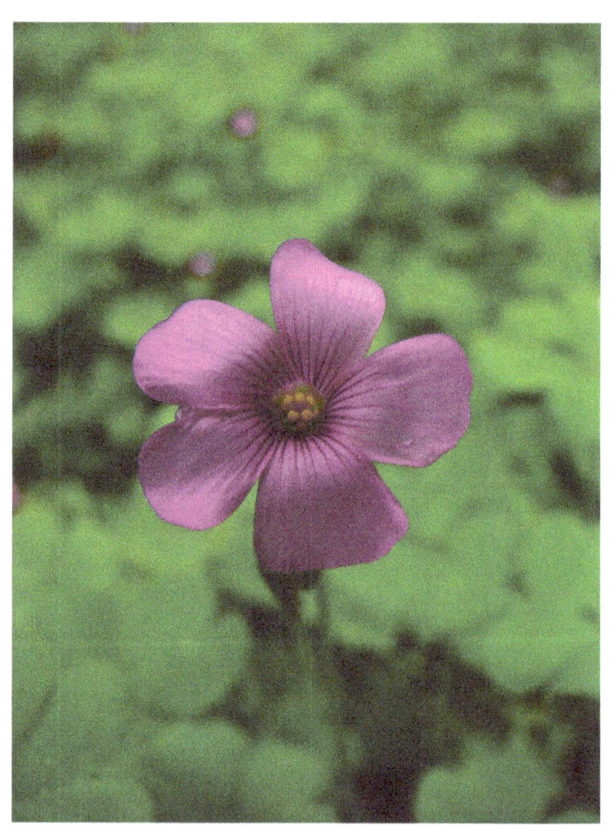

All petals are dear
Missing one would be a shear
They don't bloom all year

Photo taken in 2008

Location: Hangzhou, China

Despite living off dirt, some are floral emblems.

Notice the single "pearl" on one petal?

Born Architect

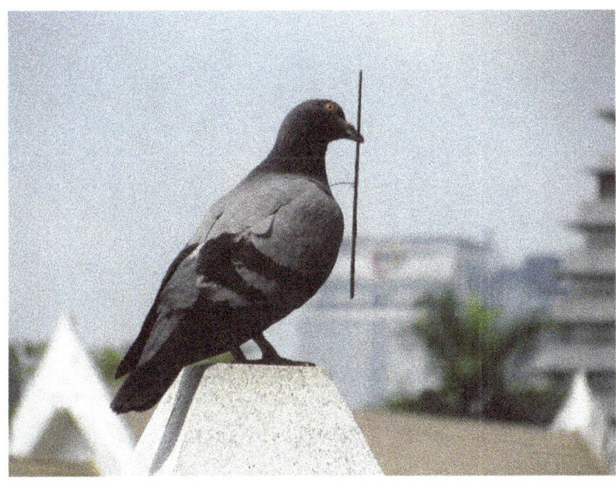

A beam holds the load
A truss for the vaulted roof
A post made of wood

Photo taken in 2013

Location: Lumpini Park, Bangkok, Thailand

It was a hot afternoon, but this hard-working pigeon
was probably taking a break. I zoomed in in order not
to startle it away. Such pose, tilted gaze with a stick
in the beak, doesn't happen often. The juxtaposing blur background
offers a contrast to my subject. Made my day.

Bridge

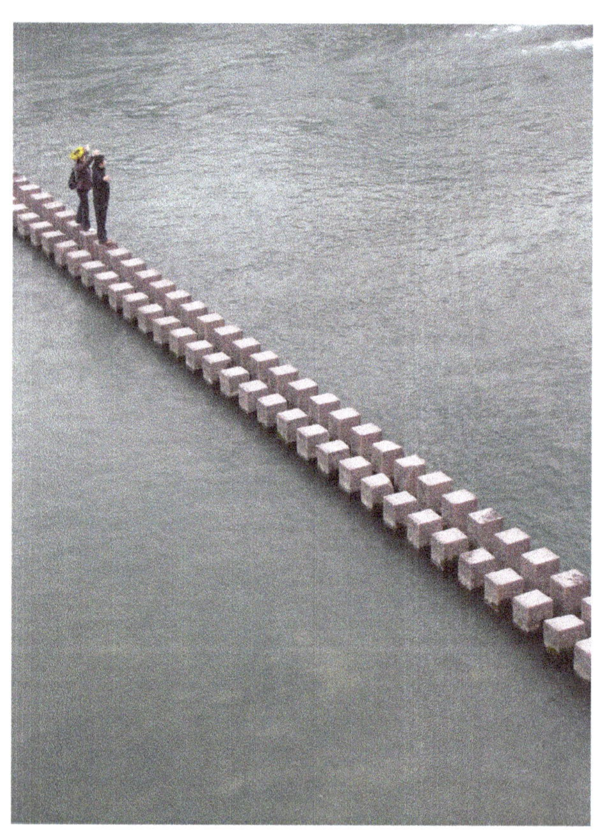

Be it a crossing
Or metaphor for linking
A path worth thanking

Photo taken in 2008

Location: Fenghuang, China

One of a kind indeed, this bridge is.

Carefree

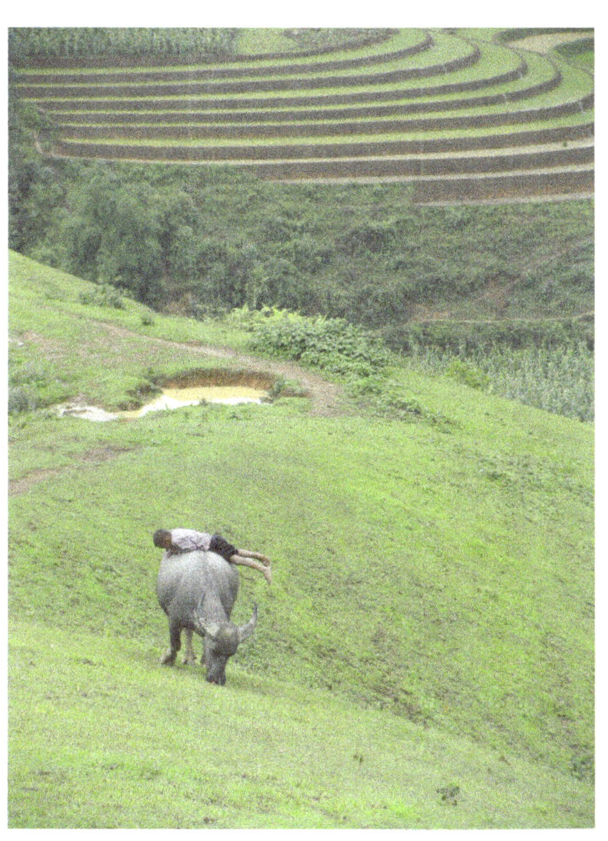

In simplicity
Joy and peace in harmony
Wouldn't you hop with glee

Photo taken in 2010

Location: Somewhere in Sa Pa, Vietnam

It was early in the morning.

As the mountain mist began to thin out,

a young buffalo rider emerged on this verdant slope.

Chained Beauty

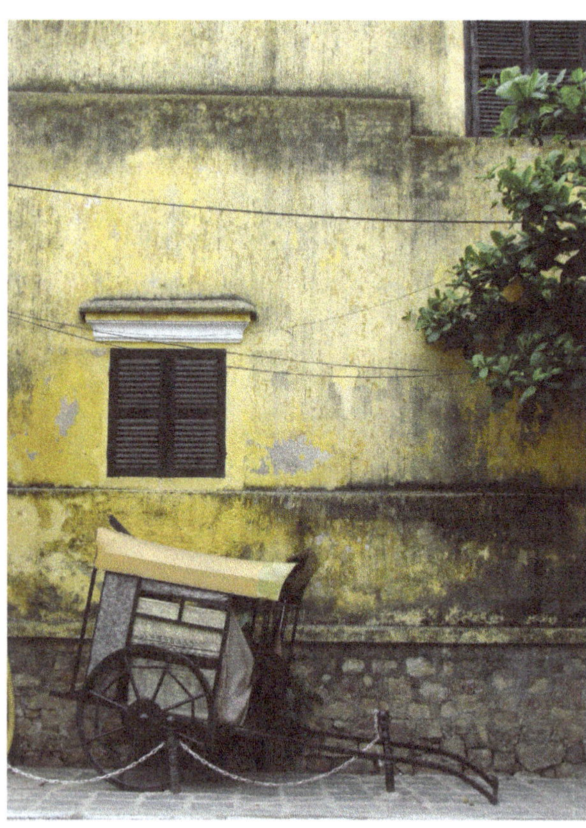

Rickshaw not for hire
As the wheels have got no tire
For one to admire

Photo taken in 2010

Location: Hoi An, Vietnam

Apart from the complementing colour scheme,

it is almost like a painting.

Ever wonder why it is called rickshaw?

Circle of Life

From one side you rise
End of day you compromise
Dawn shall re-apprise

Photo taken in 2012

Location: Senggigi, Indonesia

A sunset with drama needs a cloudy sky. This is photographers' busy time as the display is brief where the sun's gradual setting into the horizon is noticeable by the heartbeat. I took several shots. Each one offers its own shifting tone. I like this one for its tiny amber near the corner, where one cannot deny it as the focal point.

Composure

Is poise nature's gift
Striding easy narrative
Graceful persuasive

Photo taken in 2013

Location: Kovalam, India

My first day upon arrival, I almost went back to the airport. No hotel wanted me. Some said they were full. Some said no. People who arrived after me checked into the ones that said full. Of course the reception said they had pre-booked, but they asked the same question as mine, "Do you have a room?" I was exhausted running around looking for a place to stay, I would not see the room first anymore, I just wanted a room, any room. My endurance, and patience, were being pingponged from door to door, from street to street, I began to demand reason instead of a room. The hotel I could afford were not licensed to take foreign guests. My anger subsided, appreciation took over, I marched on with new spirit. I am glad I did not go back to the airport.

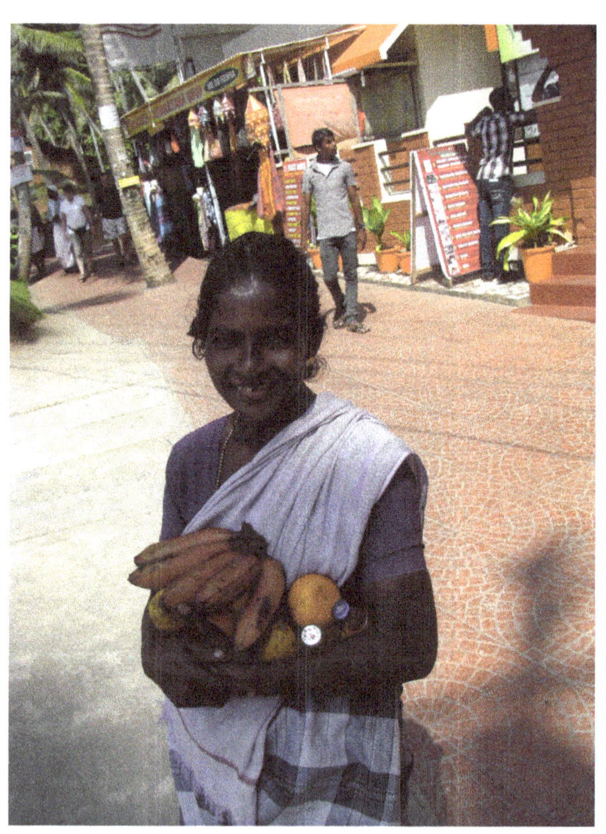

Comradery

Together we stand
In comradery we lend hand
To bond beforehand

Photo taken in 2013

Location: Echo Point, Kerala, India

I literally ran down the river bank, just in time to click,
only foreground and background defined. Simplicity.

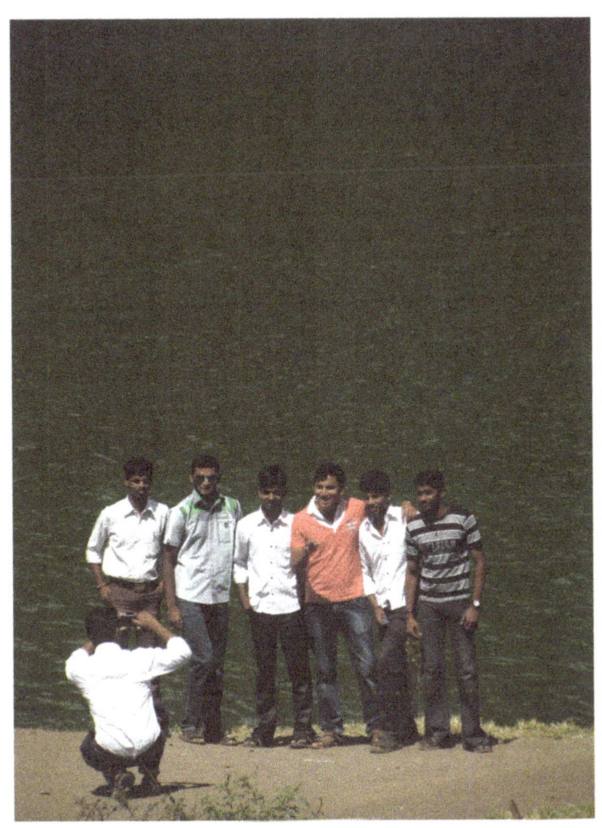

Crowd

One can be lonely
Two hugs would sure be dandy
This crowd is happy

Photo taken in 2018

Location: Cappadocia, Turkey

Two in the mornin',

my first dream was to begin,

which bed I was in

And dark was the night,

being hauled to the launch site,

to doze for day light.

Partially woke up,

the balloons had lifted up,

hush-hush, too, was up.

The wind does the rest,

drifting northwest or southwest,

hillcrest to hillcrest.

Bird's eye view's the best

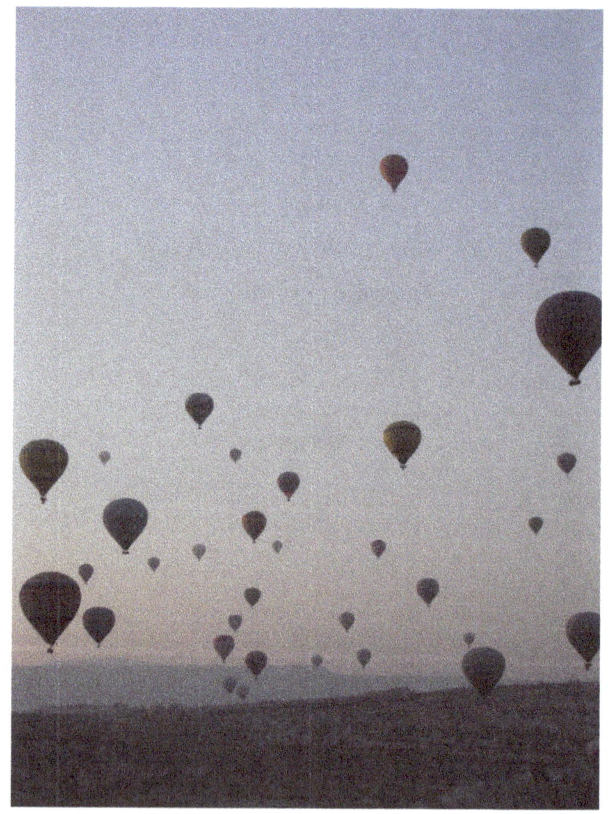

Dash

Hunting and fleeing
Everyday a ground-breaking
Survive by dashing

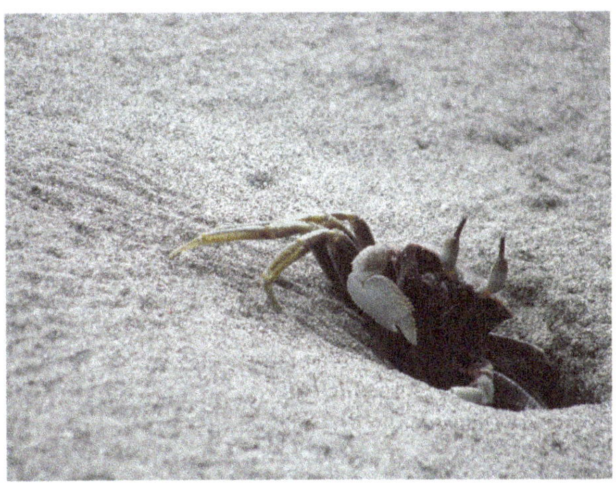

Photo taken in 2012

Location: Senggigi, Indonesia

It was a quiet morning,

the sea was calm,

but the shore was busy,

tons of these creatures,

running around in search of food,

fast as darts.

It took me several attempts,

I waited at the doorstep,

beauty stopped to check me out.

There!

Daytime Only

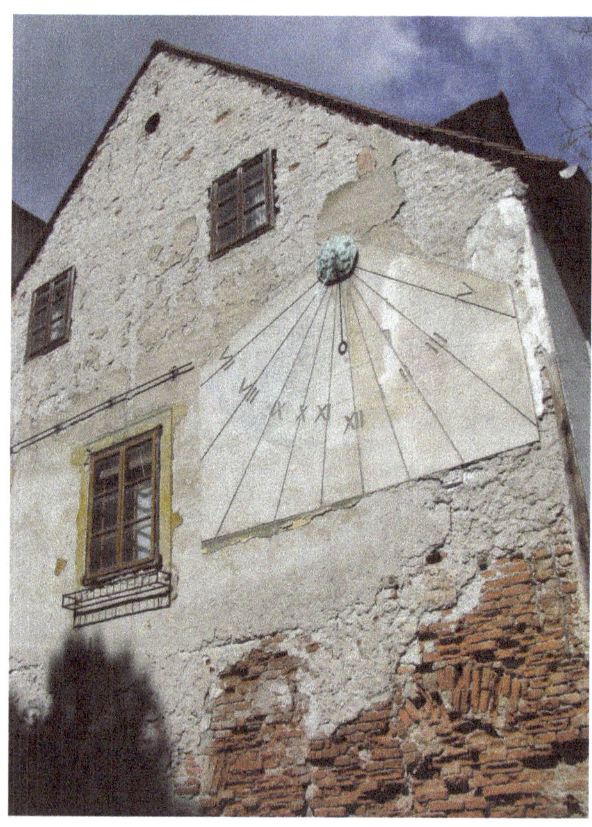

Ruined dream in midday
Grumpy owl complained away
Postman came today

Photo taken in 2017

Location: Zagreb, Croatia

A northern wall sundial must be on a south-facing wall (toward the equator). The shadow now points to noon in Zagreb whose latitude is about 45° north; displaying from 7am to 5pm with a counter-clockwise arm. At 45° in the Southern Hemisphere (on a north-facing wall, of course), the arm will move clockwise. And showtime will be backward from 5pm to 7am. Wouldn't it be nice if we could turn back the clock?

Describing Haiku

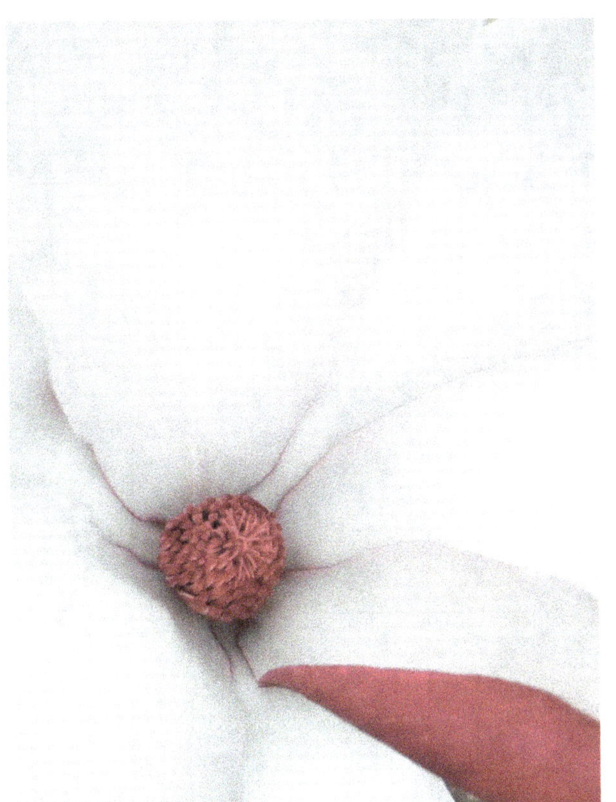

Three lines together
In seventeen syllables
Five, seven, and five

Haiku does not rhyme
It has to do with nature
Simple yet profound

They may come in pairs
Complementing each other
Sometime as triplets

Photo taken in 2022

Location: Utsunomiya, Japan

This is the inside of a flower.

From the fold of one of the petals,

you can imagine how different the exterior is.

Desert Nomad

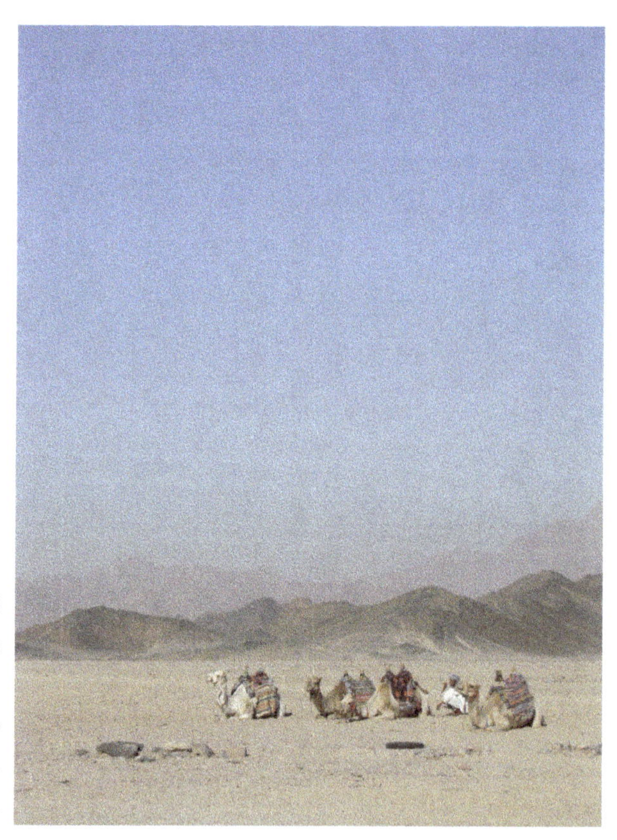

Proven throughout time
Old to young along the line
Sun wind sand are fine

Photo taken in 2016

Location: A Bedouin community in the Sahara Desert, Egypt

When nothing goes wasted,

when dung turns fuel,

resourcefulness is a prerequisite.

Design Concept

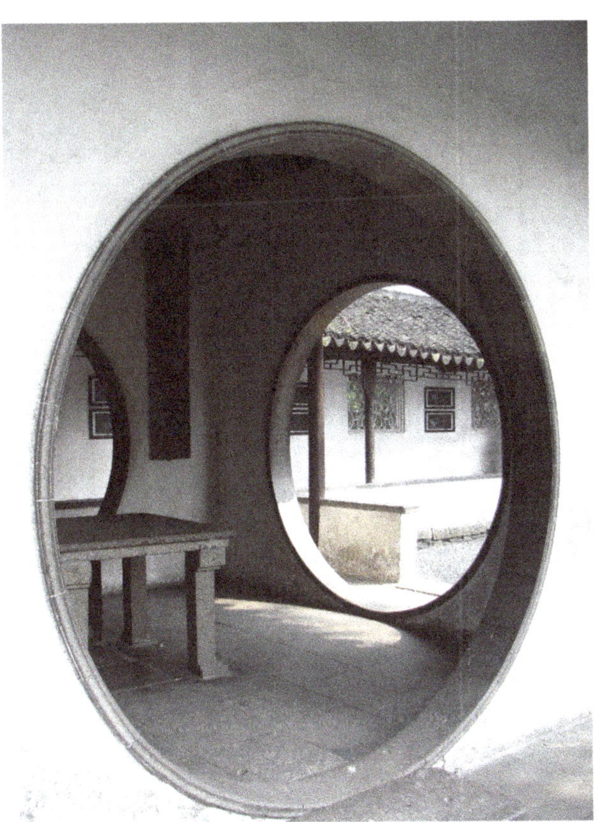

To bring inside out
Blending is all it's about
One begins to doubt

To bring outside in
Ambiguity within
Where does it begin

Photo taken in 2008

Location: Suzhou, China

To make a small room feel large is to create an impression that it is part of the outside, thus the design concept of bringing the outside in (or vice versa). For example, interior and exterior floors/walls share the same pattern/material, hence, creatng an "ambiguity" between in and out. As a result, if done effectively, psychological spatial expansion can happen through perception without physically enlarging it.

Devotion

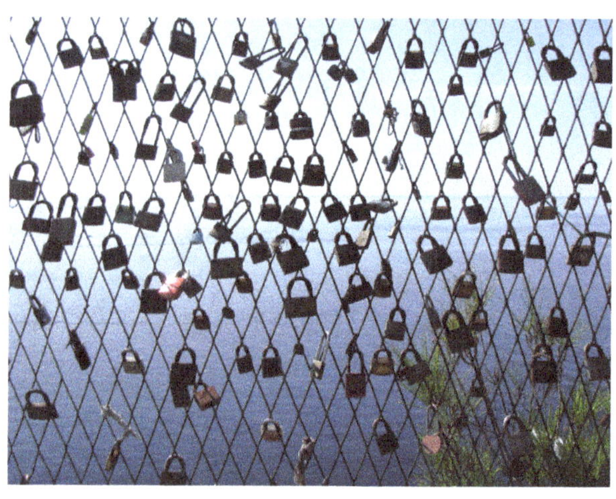

In contemplation
A zeal of dedication
Pledging devotion

Photo taken in 2017

Location: Dubrovnik, Croatia

Perched high on a steep cliff,

overlooking the deep blue below,

this safety fence becomes a novelty.

Accordingly, the keys of these locks were thrown into the sea.

Dew Want-to-be

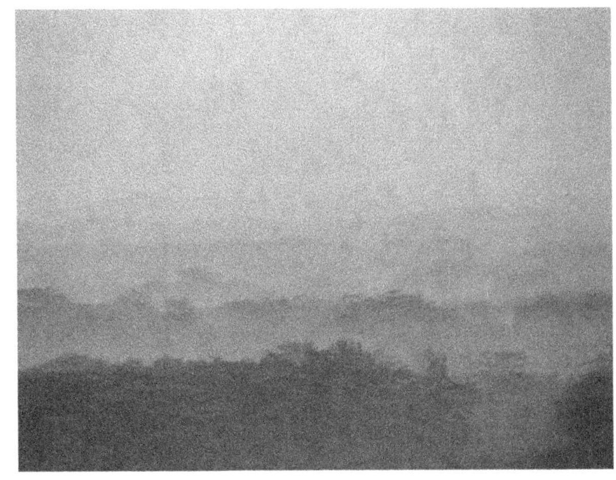

Sweeping horizon
Moisture ribbon by ribbon
The dawn has broken

Photo taken in 2008

Location: Bukit Batok, Singapore

Sometimes a gloomy day can be a blessing in disguise,

DIDO

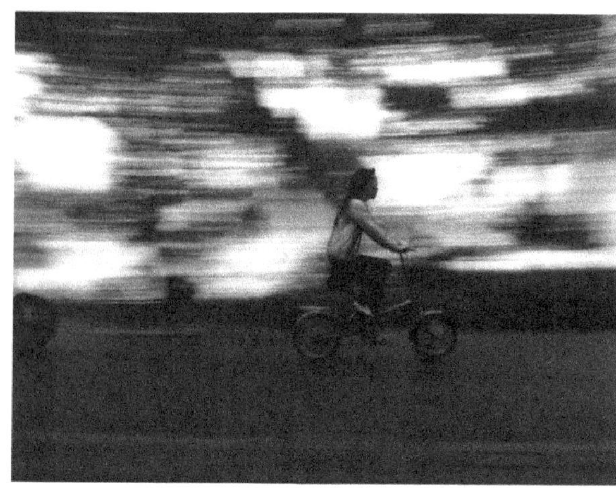

Day in and day out
Sorting this and that about
Forgot to logout

Photo taken in 2008

Location: Hangzhou, China

Panning to follow a moving subject with your camera

while taking the shot is challenging but fun.

More information about panning:

<https://www.adobe.com/creativecloud/photography/discover/panning-photography.html>

Downstream Price

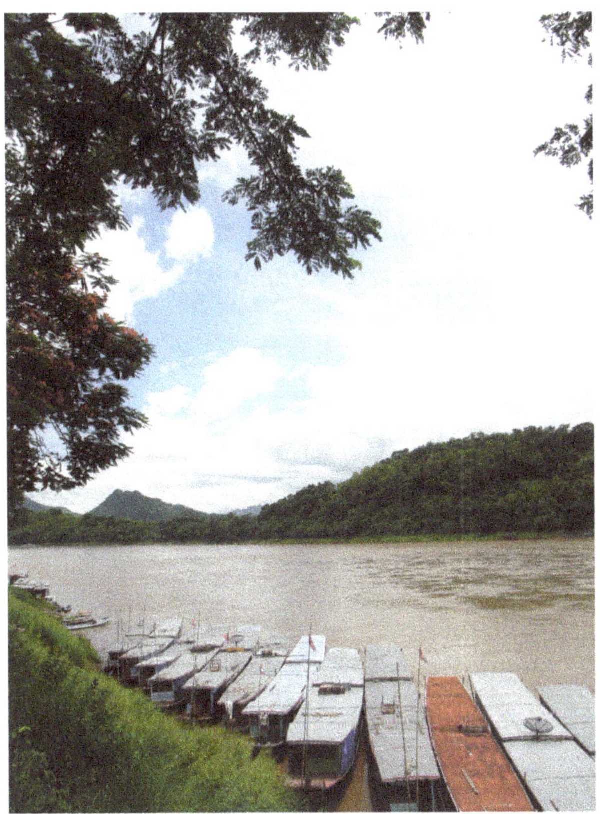

No paddling in fact
But save it for the way back
A price for the slack

Photo taken in 2010

Location: Mekong River, Luang Prabang, Laos

We are looking downstream, wouldn't you reckon? Do you also know that from its source on the Tibetan Plateau to the Mekong Delta, how many countries does this river flow through?

To track real-time water level and flood warning of Mekong River: <https://portal.mrcmekong.org/monitoring/river-monitoring-telemetry>

Drop by

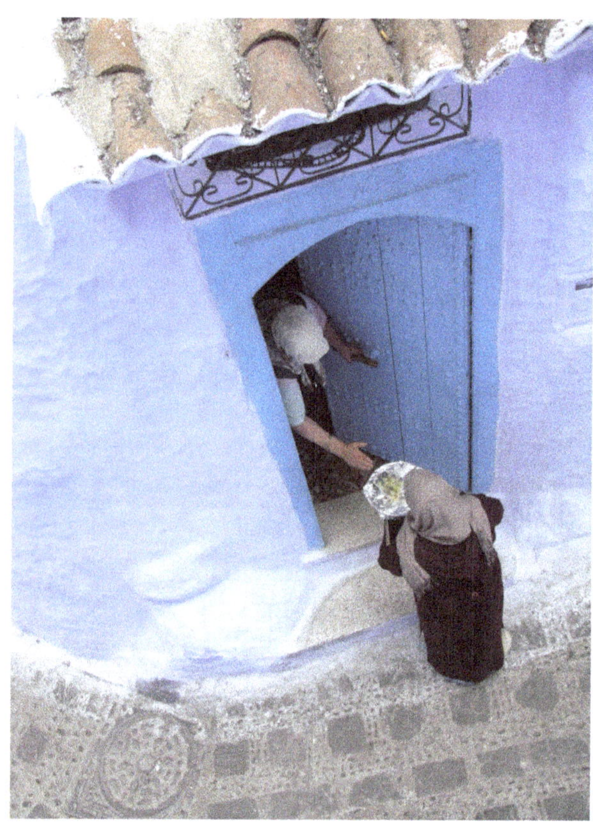

Take and give keystone
Where all streets are cobblestoned
As friendship is honed

Photo taken in 2018

Location: Chefchaouen, Morocco

The woman in the house was aware of this photo.

She looked up and saw me before closing the door.

Early Bird

On the ledge I perch
Above abyss I shall search
A worm near the birch

Photo taken in 2020
Location: Krabi, Thailand

I wanted to play with "visual obligation" toward the corner by placing the focal point far from the expected central location within the frame.
Do you think it was achieved?

Echoes

Pattern unfading
From balconies to railings
Shadows agreeing

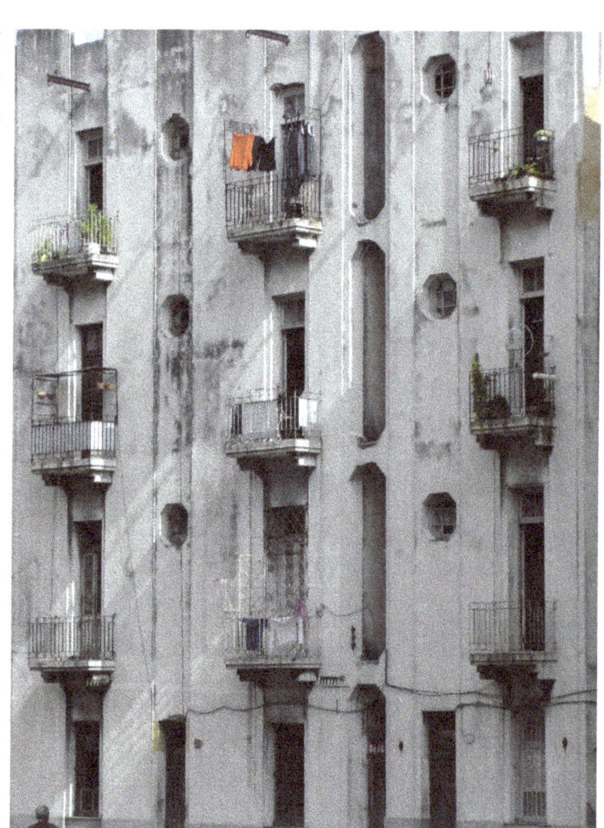

Photo taken in 2010

Location: Havana, Cuba

Habits develop into character.

Exploration

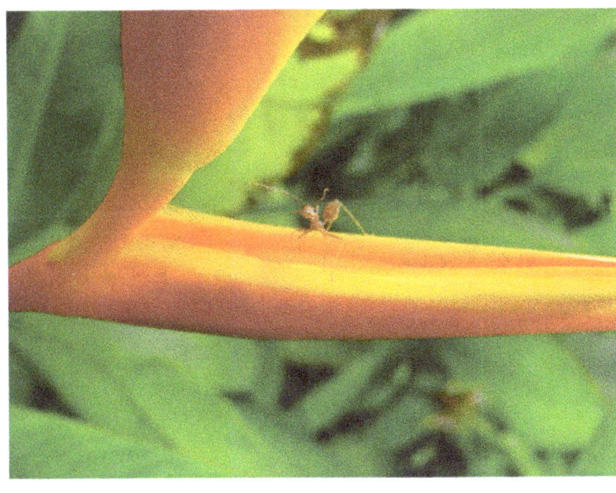

A thought in the head
Perching high up where it sat
If one dares inspect

Photo taken in 2013

Location: Chatuchak Park, Bangkok, Thailand

This little creature is not only fast, but also agile.

It disappeared the same time as my camera clicked.

Notice that it is almost as orange as the flower.

Do you think the "camouflage" is a defense mechanism?

Explore both worlds, the one in our heads and the one around us.

Eye Contact

The thoughts behind looks
What visual cue that one took
Not found in the book

Photo taken in 2013

Location: Kovalam, India

To meet the world with defiance is courage.

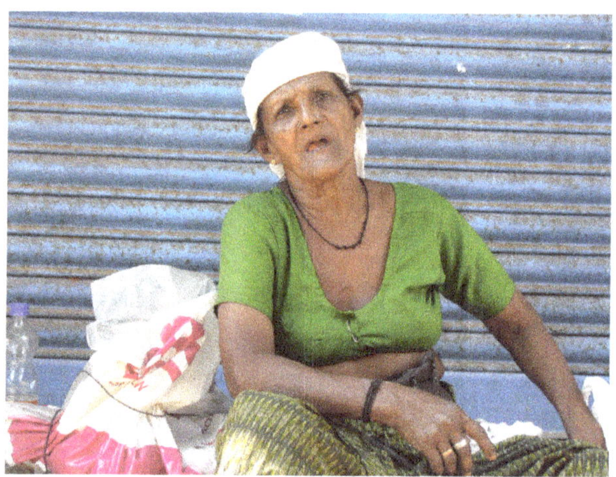

Faith

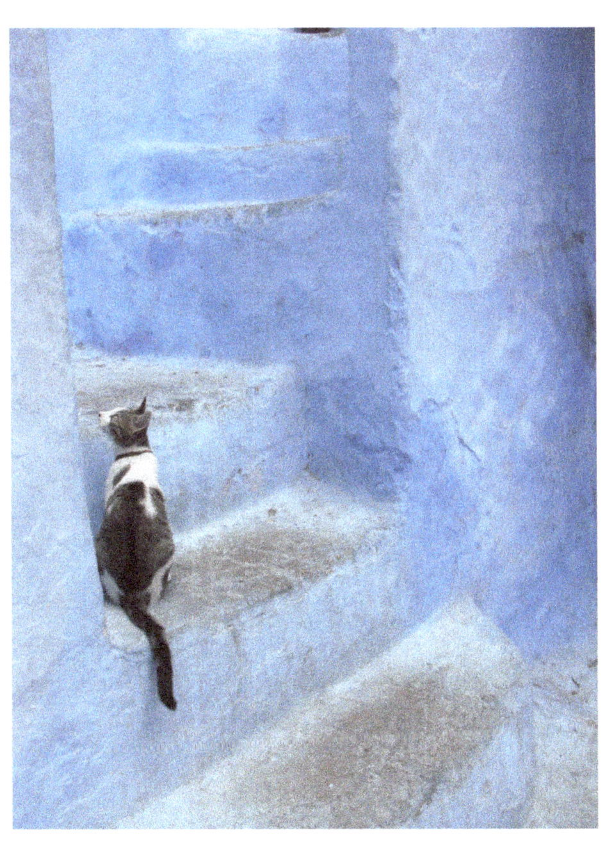

A future to face
Not seeing the whole staircase
First step taken place

Photo taken in 2018

Location: Chefchaouen, Morocco

This shot was pure luck, both in time and place.

Fibonacci Curve

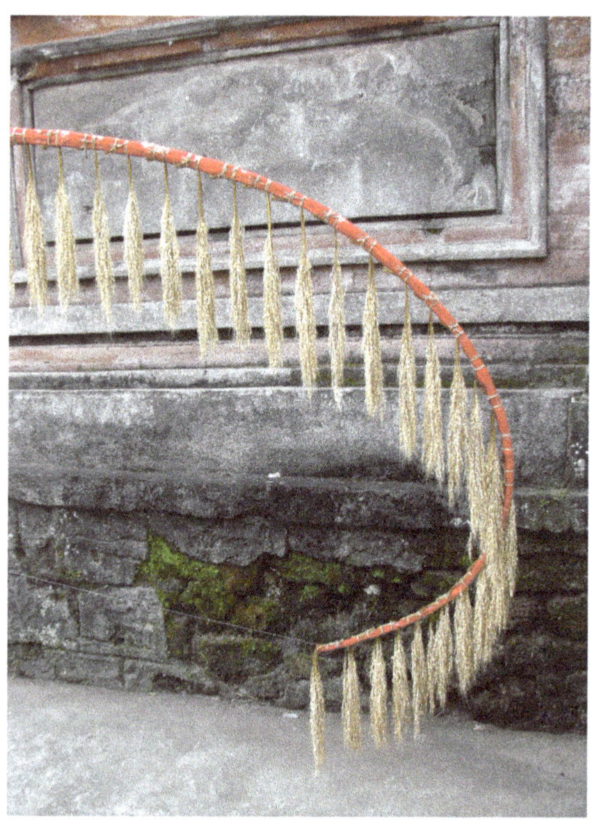

Straight roads see distance
Curve lines conjure elegance
In curves live tension

Photo taken in 2012

Location: Ubud, Indonesia

Each village has its own style, I did not make this *penjor* (street decoration made of bamboo and rice), but I did take part in tying one up for the *galungan* (Balinese festival). When erected, along both sides of the streets, they look like rice paddy ready for harvest, hence every *penjor* curves to reflect this moment.

Forward Backward

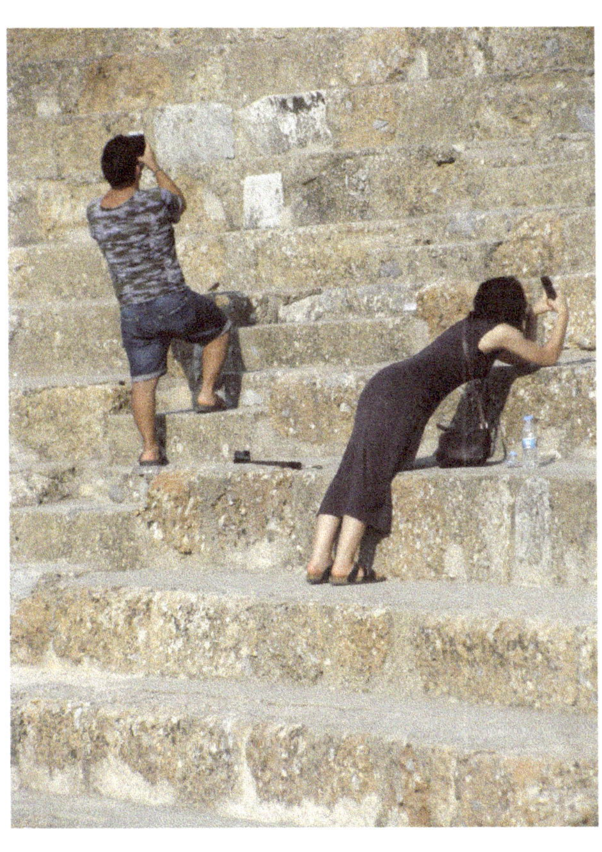

Welcome spectators
Greeted the stage announcer
Seated spectators

To the spectators
Somehow backstage they prefer
Poor stage announcer

Photo taken in 2018

Location: Hierapolis, Turkey

I looked upward, too, but saw nothing,

so I captured both of them.

Freedom

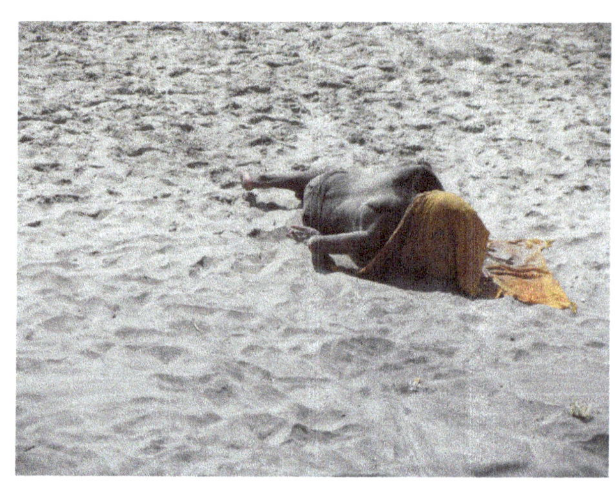

Of its own legion
Content with no possession
On self-abstention

Photo taken in 2013

Location: Kovalam, India

It was high noon and shadows were short.

The beach was quiet and baking hot.

When you close your eyes, does it step a notch up on other senses?

Germination

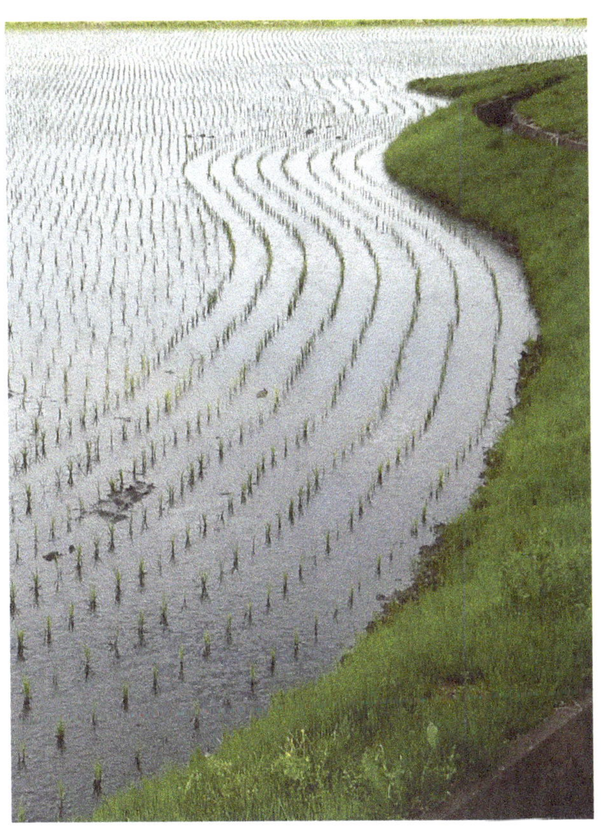

Good fruits from good seed
As trait derives from his deed
Curve or straight indeed

Photo taken in 2020

Location: Utsunomiya, Japan

From the pattern, the rice seedlings are no longer planted manually?

Gestures

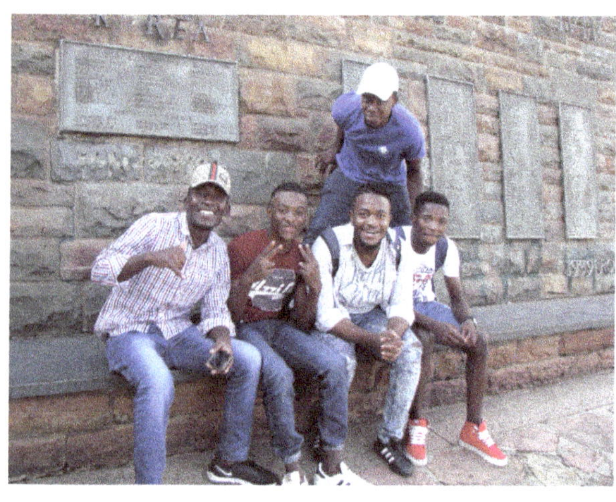

Some universal
Across cultures and people
Sharing hand signal

Photo taken in 2018

Location: Pretoria, South Africa

It started from the two on the left making gestures, then the third joined in,

then the fourth, and the fifth is trying to squeeze in somewhere, there were seven of them.

I chose this one because of the "nowhere to squeeze-in look".

(Trivia: GESTURES in Morse code --. . ... - ..- .-. . ...)

Golden Key

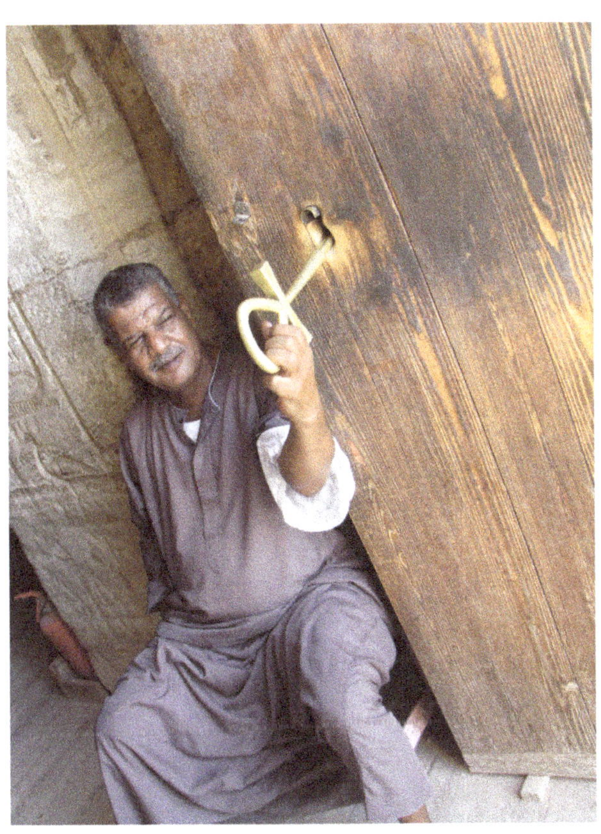

Where to draw the line
What is yours and what is mine
Trust earned is divine

Photo taken in 2016

Location: Abu Simbel, Egypt

Around the key hole, witnesses the wear and tear of time, golden as the key.

Gone Fishing

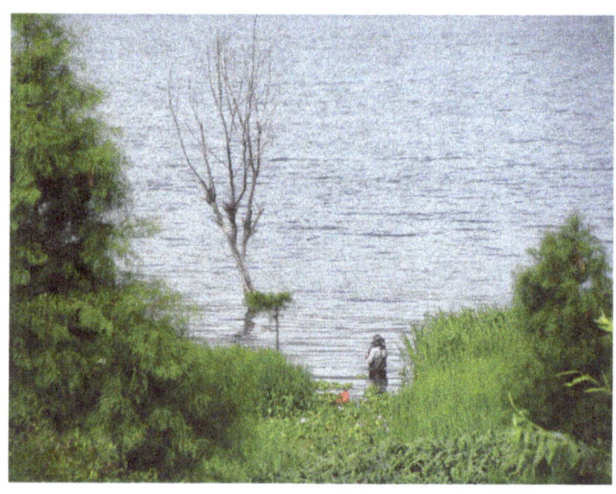

Photo taken in 2018

Location: Dali, China

Time wasted is well-spent when you have fun,

especially when the soul is nurtured.

Know you've done your best
If you need to take a break
Know you deserve it

(Inspired by fellow teachers during teachers' stress relief session)

Good Things Come in Threes

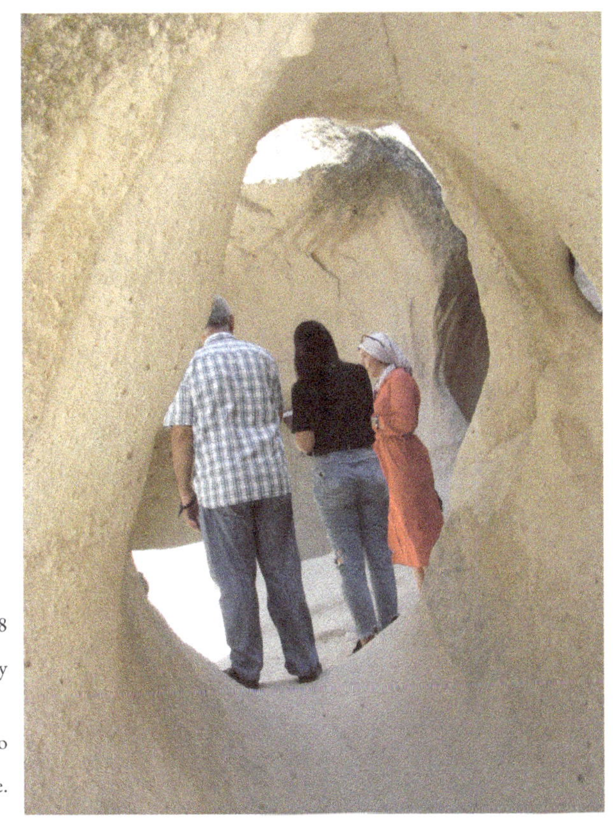

When friendship's cherished
Where inner peace is nourished
With dream accomplished

Photo taken in 2018

Location: Göreme, Turkey

I like the colour scheme that is happening here, complementing hues to the earthy yet unearthly landscape.

Graffiti

Must be close to home
When street voice has matching tone
What is there to hone

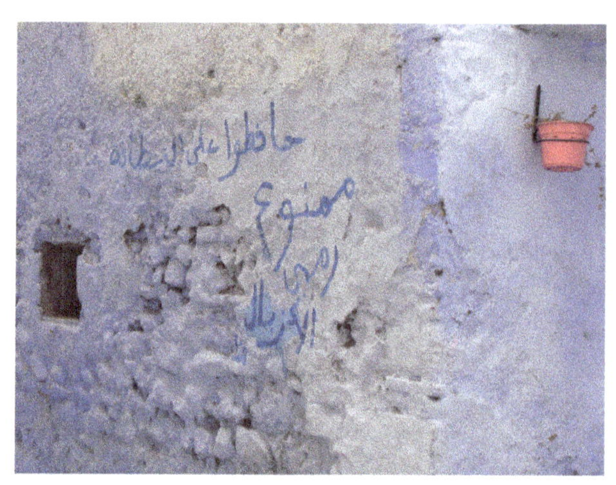

Photo taken in 2018

Location: Chefchaouen, Morocco

Only a small pot plant and a small window on the wall,

but in some architectural approach, less is more,

it allows imagination to play,

to perceive, and to conclude.

Grain Grind Ground

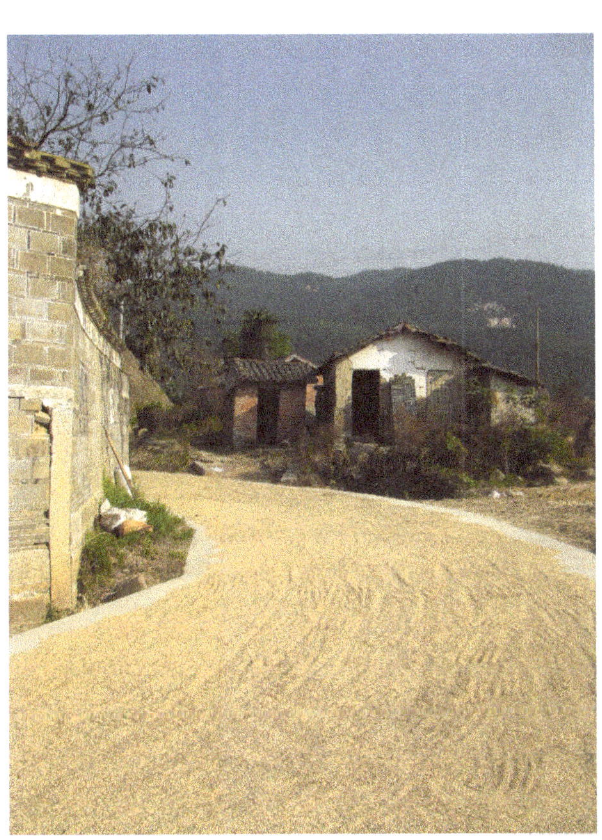

Farmers toil the soil
Strong wind can bring a turmoil
Rain may lurk to spoil

Harvest brings me thrill
To be crunched before the till
An improvised mill

Photo taken in 2008

Location: Somewhere in Jiangxi, China

The rural bus had no bus stop. I had a name of a village. Didn't know where to get off. Driver not sure. Other passenger said, "Get off here."

So, I did.

Hierarchy

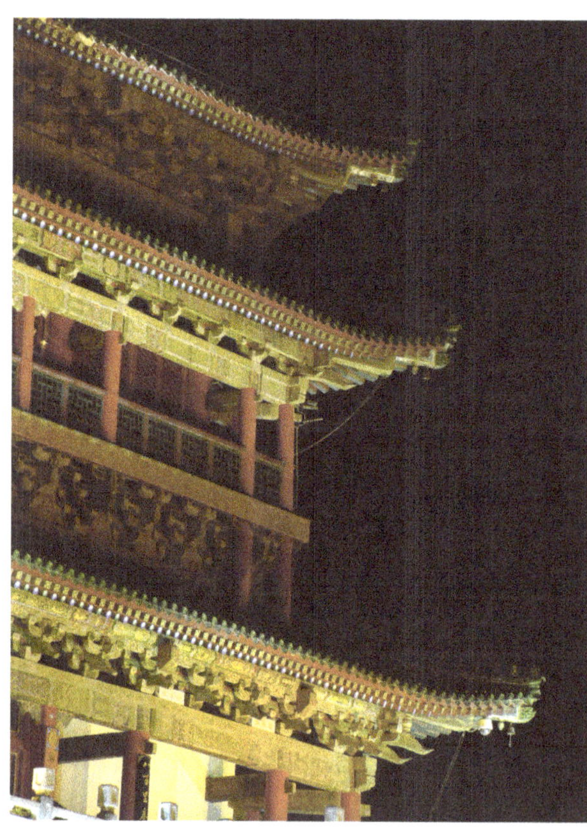

From the commoners
To the administrators
Under emperors

Photo taken in 2008

Location: Bell Tower, Xi'an, China

Hierarchy is like a tree,

standing on its roots,

trunk to hold up the crown.

Hollowness

Material released
With no desire to appease
To find inner peace

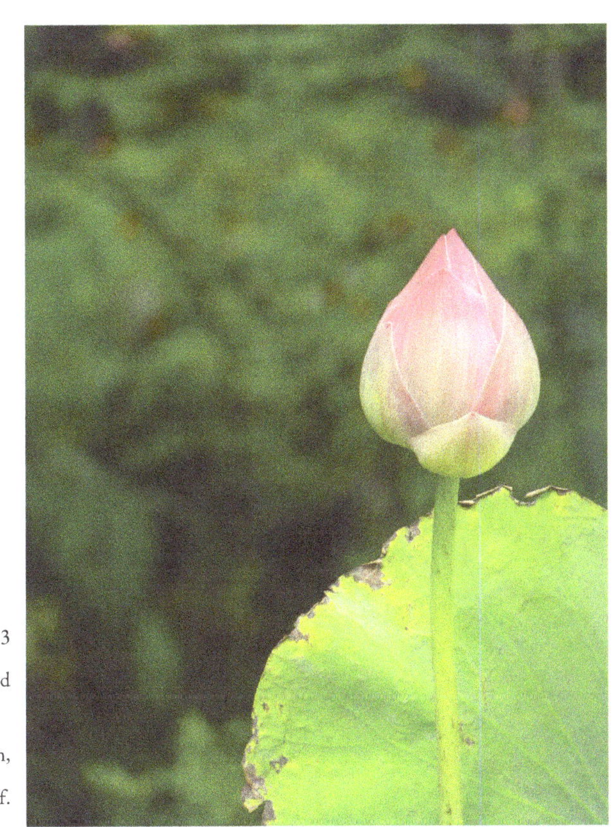

Photo taken in 2013

Location: Chatuchak Park, Bangkok, Thailand

At first I thought it would be perfect if the entire leaf were green,
but the more I look at it, the more it offers natural truth about itself.

If I were a Child

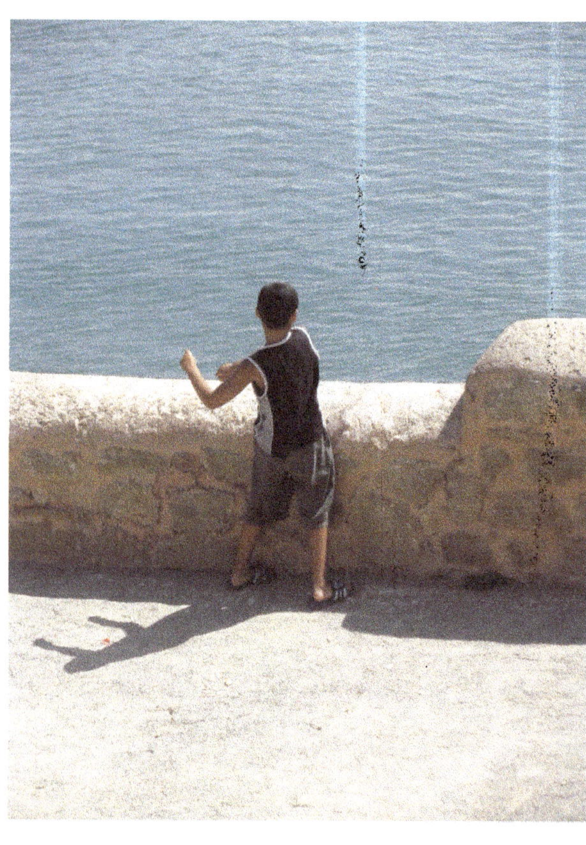

If I were a child
Innocence is my lifestyle
Only for awhile

Now that I look back
I wish that I could go back
To have a playback

Photo taken in 2018

Location: Qasbat al-Awdāya, Rabat, Morocco

A carefree world, the world envies.

If I were a Fisherman

For it's a custom
To find to catch to come home
Grant me the wisdom

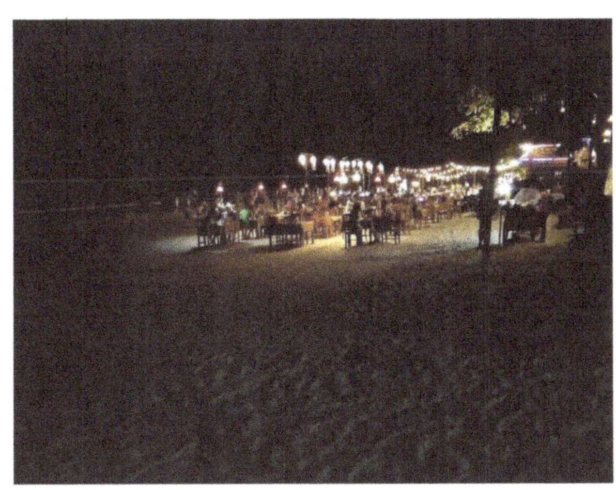

Photo taken in 2019

Location: Koh Samet, Thailand

I were a fisherman,

this is probably my front yard;

perhaps dimmer.

Gazing stars on moist warm sand,

listening to the receding tides,

having the fish I caught today,

I will repeat tomorrow.

The stars shall guide me home.

If I were a fisherman.

If I were a Horse

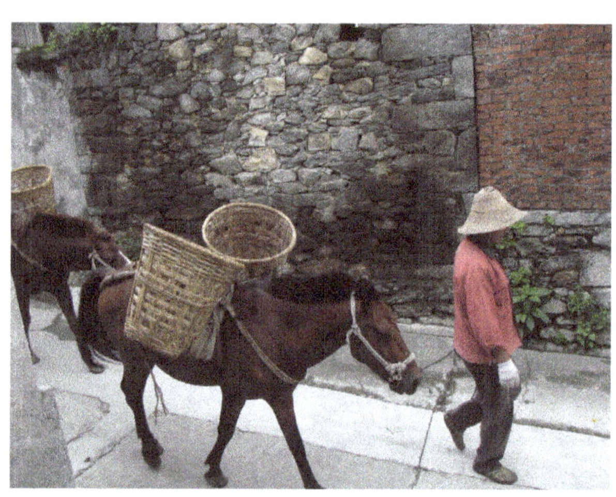

For my endurance
Historical evidence
Battleground preference

A graceful creature
For therapy and nurture
Also for pleasure

Photo taken in 2018

Location: Dali, China

Working pony says

Having a sore throat he prays

I'm a little hoarse

If I were a Prey

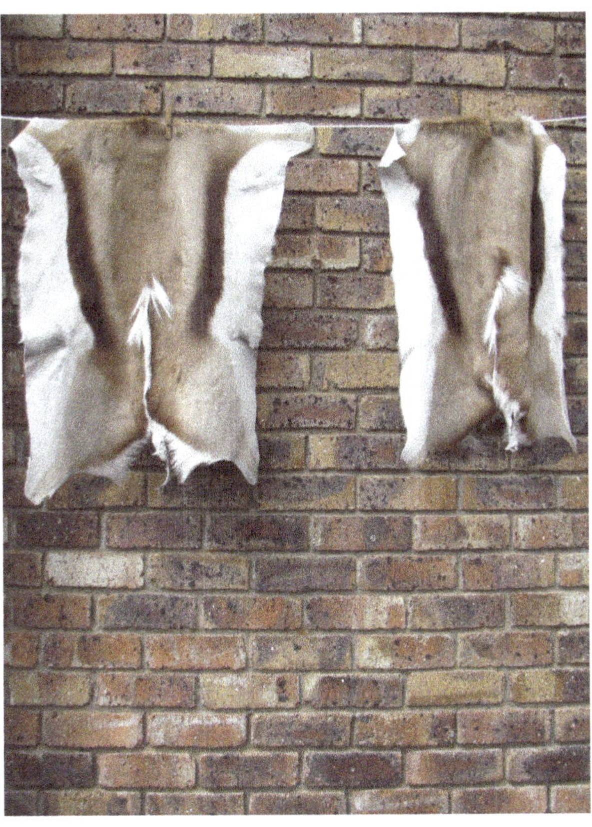

The meek gets eaten
While predators get beaten
Before flesh rotten

Photo taken in 2018

Location: Somewhere in South Africa

The curved optic distortion of the brick line at the bottom,
I didn't notice at the time, wouldn't have occurred had the
camera not been tilted up for this shot.

If I were a Worm

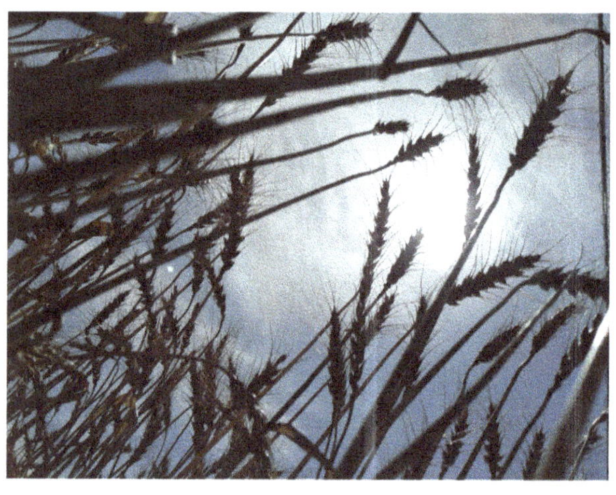

In soil came a squirm
Tomorrow's nutrients affirmed
If I were a worm

Photo taken in 2020

Location: Utsunomiya, Japan

In architecture, presentation is routine, showing different perspective of a design, idea or concept.

There is bird's eye view from the top, eye-level view, and worm's eye view looking up.

Looking up to appreciate grandeur, to admire magnificence...and here, just to be grateful to nature's provisions.

Inner Peace

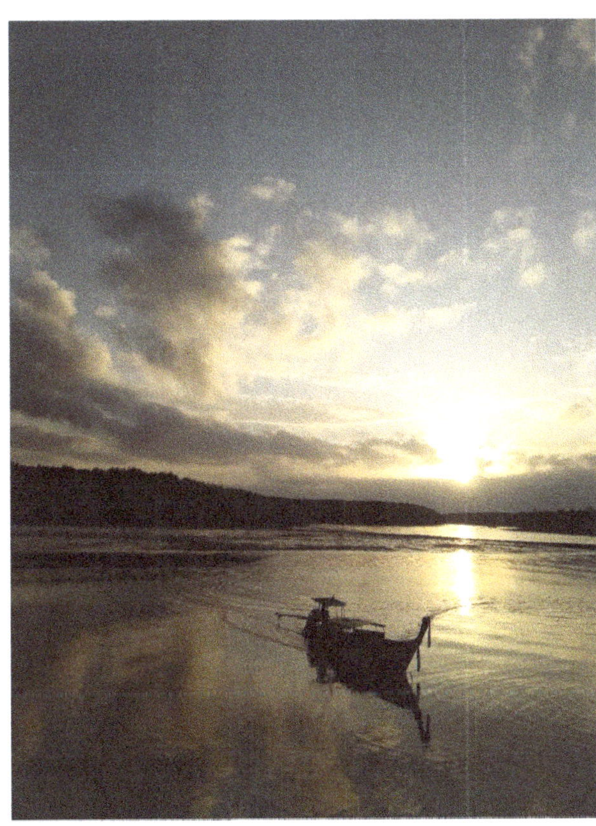

Where do I begin
Comfortable under own skin
None to lose nor win

Photo taken in 2020

Location: Krabi River, Thailand

I was stranded here when COVID-19 struck. I came to this riverside often to contemplate in tranquility and uncertainty. Despite being a night owl, dawn was my preferred time to be at this spot, just peaceful moment.

Instinct

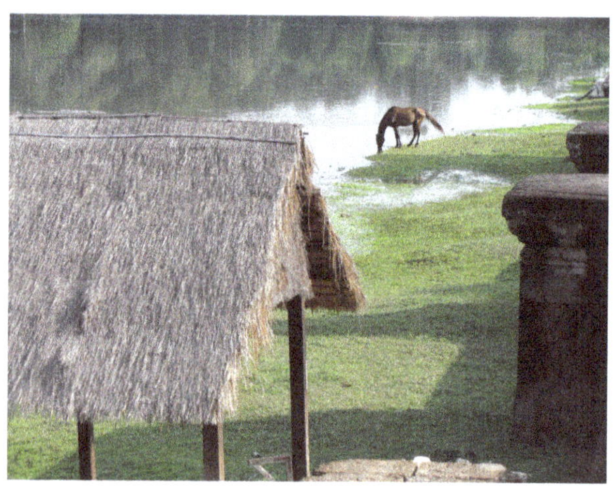

The minds can play tricks
The heart feels that it should leap
Instinct you can't beat

Photo taken in 2010

Location: The moat of Angkor Wat, near Siem Reap, Cambodia

Animal instinct, we don't have.

Worrying about bad things, we do have;

which can hinder us from enjoying the good things.

Into the Horizon

What tomorrow rings
Whether they are hopes or dreams
The journey begins

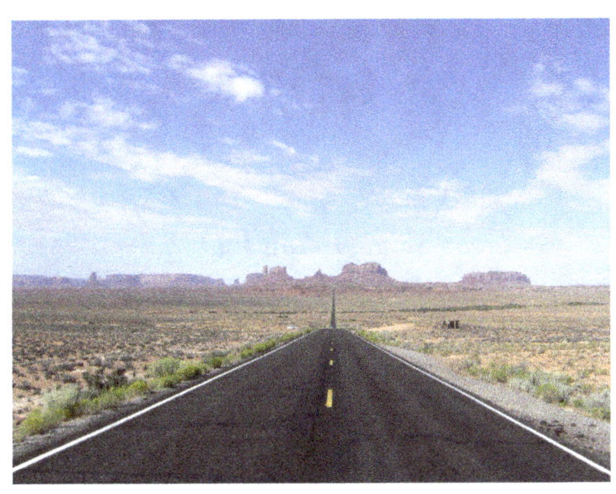

Photo taken in 2007

Location: Navajo Monument Valley (Utah-Arizona), U.S.A.

Time heals and erodes,

the soul and the flesh.

Hold the moment in your palm.

Inukshuk in Africa

Solid ground I stand
Onto horizon I plan
As best as I can

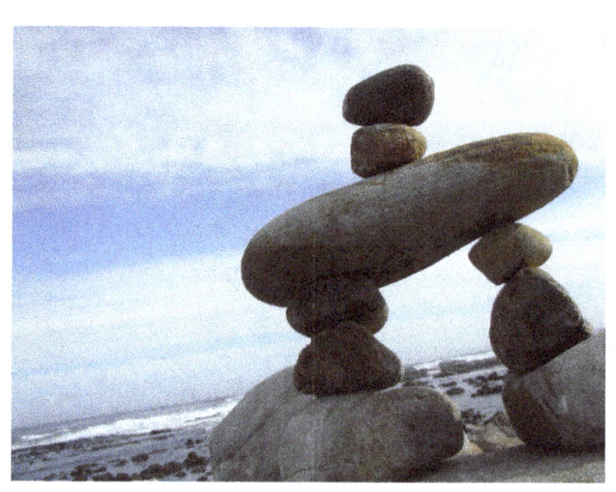

Photo taken in 2018

Location: Cape of Good Hope, South Africa

I built this *inukshuk* (or *inuksuk*) out of impulse,

inspired by the elongated rocks scattered around.

A real *inukshuk* in northern Canada would function as a landmark.

More information about *inukshuk*:

<https://www.thecanadianencyclopedia.ca/en/article/inuksuk-inukshuk>

Kite Train

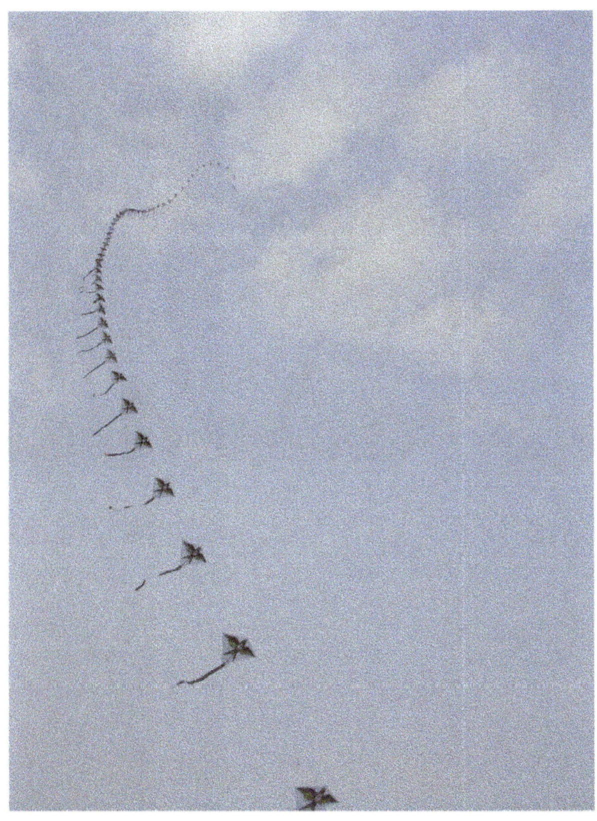

Released from the reel
Serenity wants to heal
Calm and peaceful feel

Photo taken in 2008

Location: Xi'an, China

It was the first time I saw kite train. I used to make my own "combat" kites (with no tail for agility; tails stabilize them) as a child where I would compete with other kites, to cut each other's kite off; it's a sport, no hard feelings. A well-constructed kite and a skilled flyer can perform aerobatic stunts, from any degree of sudden sharp turns (including 180° reverse) to somersaults, and you can "write and draw" in the sky. No one got famous for it, just for fun.

Knocker

A half opened door
A temptation to explore
Will it be a lure

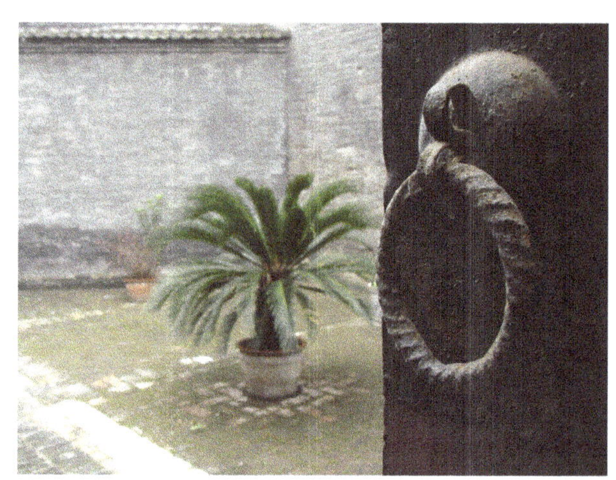

Photo taken in 2008

Location: Xi'an, China

Today saw yesterday, tomorrow will see today.

Lantern from Heaven

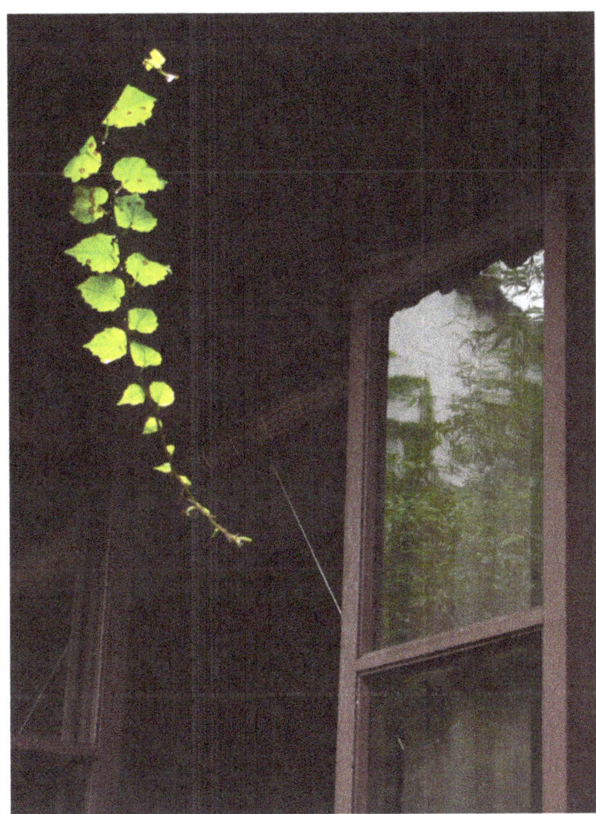

When the day is gloom
Should one stop to smell the bloom
Pond'ring what to groom

Photo taken in 2008

Location: Hangzhou, China

My bus arrived at night, hungry and tired, I walked in search of accommo-
dation. Following pointers' directions, back and forth I repeatedly passed
by one dark parking lot. Frustrated and almost gave up, I ventured into the
dark parking lot and found a gravel footpath leading to my bed. The next
day, in combing the vicinity in the rain, I realized that I had walked into a
park in the dark without noticing lotus in the lake and weeping willow in
rhythmic sway. These leaves suspended on a stem, illuminated against the
dark shade, offers redemption that brightens the day.

Lighthouse Story

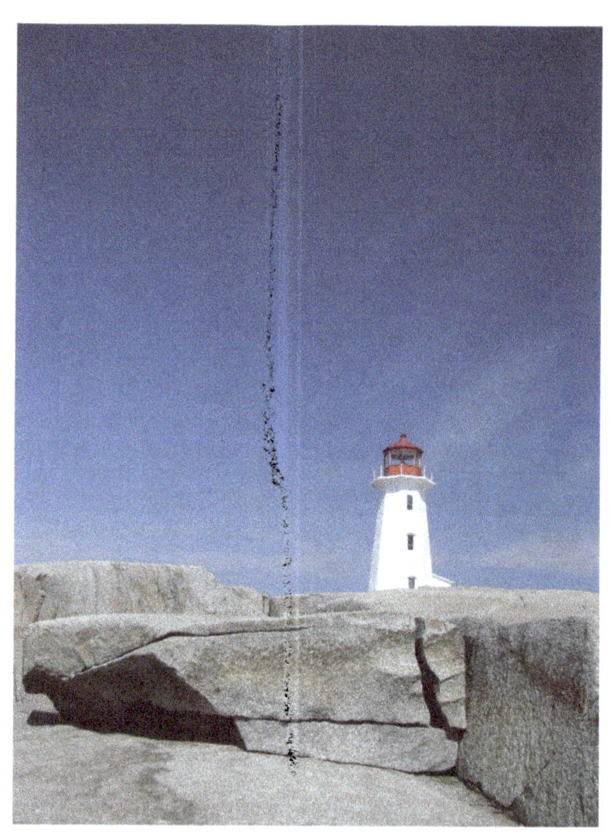

Battered and weathered
Romanticized and admired
Spirit undeterred

Stand in solitude
Gail and storm of magnitude
Tall and resolute

Photo taken in 2009

Location: Peggys Cove, Canada

This iconic lighthouse is more than just a beacon for seafarers, it is also a symbol of this small fishing community.

More information about types, roles, and history of lighthouses in Canada: <https://www.dfo-mpo.gc.ca/otw-am/lighthouses-phares/canada-eng.html>

Live off the Land

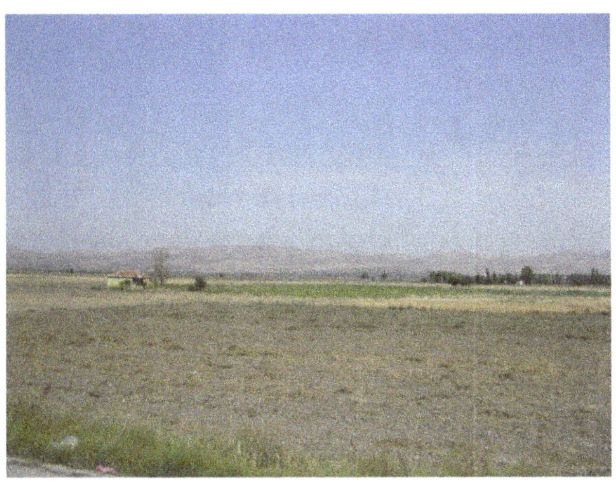

Set foot on this soil
From dawn to dusk I shall toil
What is there to foil

Photo taken in 2018

Location: Somewhere in Turkey

From a window seat, in a long haul coach,

dozing (drooling) off intermittently,

waking up to this brave lone house,

almost blending into the landscape.

Live off the Water

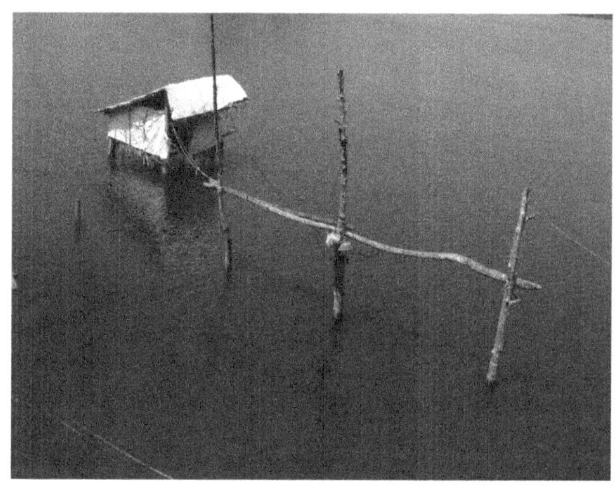

A school in the lot
In abundance swim some cod
Luxury is not

Photo taken in 2013

Location: Vypīn Island, India

I didn't know where to take the connecting bus.

I ended up walking.

I ended up here.

Water comes in forms, depending on its mood:

From the tranquil reflective mirror to the roar of the bore.

Lone River Skimmer

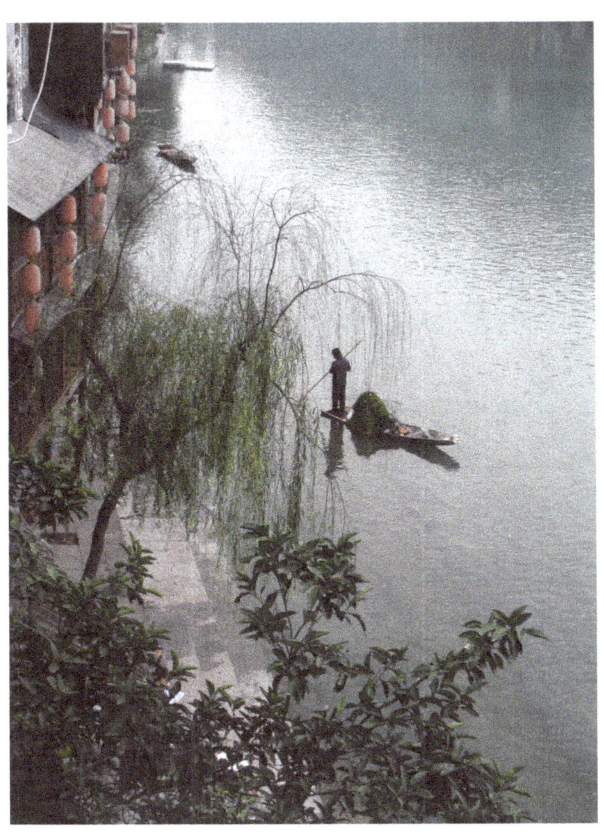

A chore seen as low
Meditation on the flow
Disguised blessing though

Photo taken in 2008

Location: Fenghuang, China

The man, using a net to scoop up algae from the river

to prevent algal bloom, which can be harmful to aquatic life.

As you can see, he has scooped up a green pile on his boat.

Long and Winding

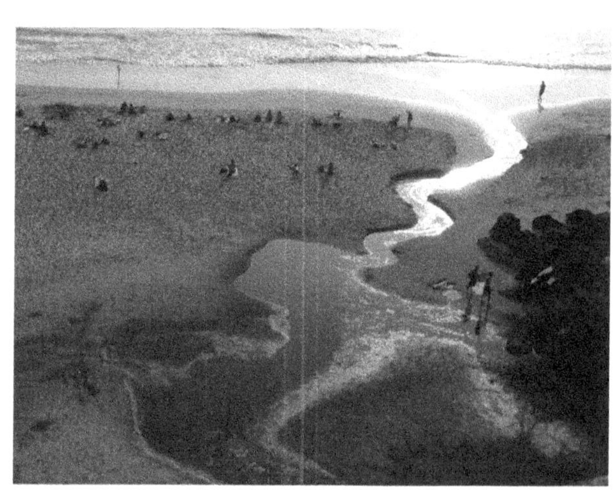

From spring to ocean
Through all terrain formations
Finding completion

Photo taken in 2013

Location: Varkala, India

When we face the sun,

our shadow falls behind us.

and light before us.

Long Tail Tale

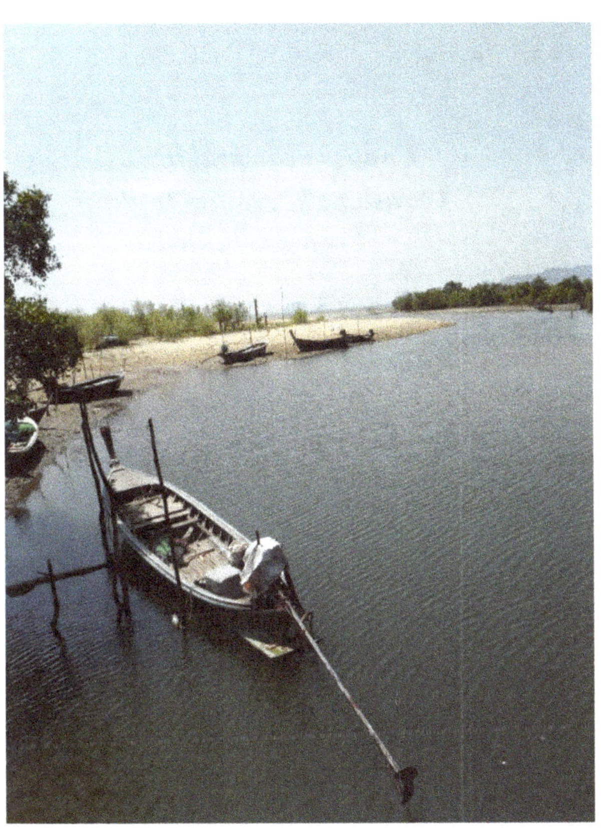

Chugging starts at dawn
Drop kids off to school I yawn
Daily chores press on

Photo taken in 2020

Location: A village in a tributary of the Krabi River, Thailand

They are called long tail boats because their propellers are mounted on a long shaft that can tilt vertically up to just below the water surface for maneuverability in shallow waters when the tide is low.

Minimalism

Canvas clean and sheen
A brushstroke renders to glean
A point to be seen

Photo taken in 2018

Location: Somewhere along the Dardanelles Strait, Turkey

There were many gulls chasing above the ferry I was on. Sometimes passengers feed them. Took a few attempts to get this one with the rule of thirds where my subject is placed about 1/3 off the edges of the frame.

More information about rule of thirds:

<https://www.nikonusa.com/en/learn-and-explore/a/tips-and-techniques/5-easy-composition-guidelines.html>

Mister Buzz

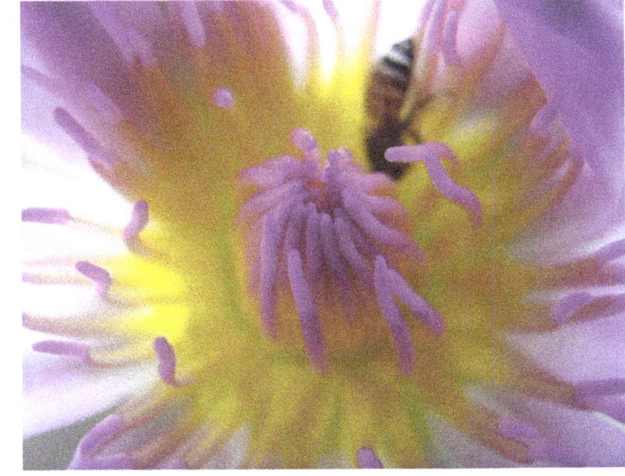

Here comes Mister Buzz
Hops here hops there makes no fuss
Nectar is a must

Photo taken in 2013

Location: Chatuchak Park, Bangkok, Thailand

I was interested in the close-up view of the shifting hues

of the tentacles when I set my camera to macro.

Mr. B was too busy to be bothered by my intrusion,

nor was I aware of my intrusion,

until after the shot was taken.

Morning Catch

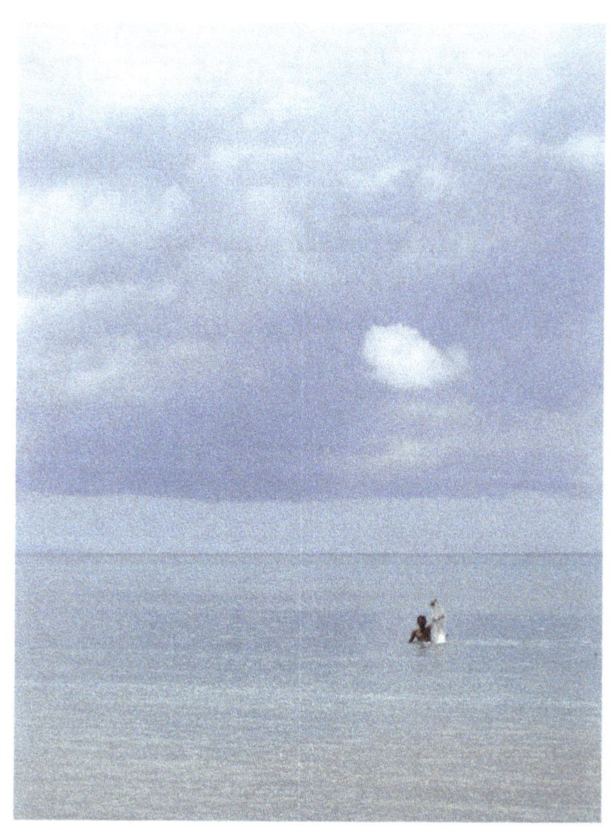

Seafood is sure fresh
When the throw's a spread out splash
There's no need for cash

Photo taken in 2012

Location: Senggigi, Indonesia

Just the fisherman and me. You can tell that the sea is shallow (10x zoom from the shore). One cloud stands out, hanging right above the man.

Mother's Greatness

Moral upbringing
Understands without saying
Trust and respecting

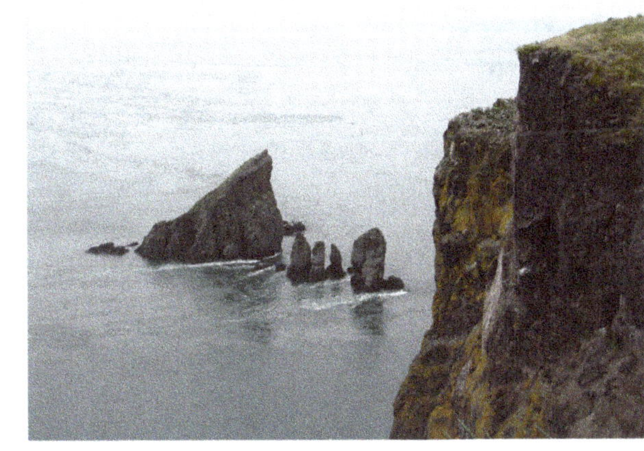

Photo taken in 2008

Location: Bay of Fundy seen from Cape Split, Canada

The basalt pinnacles jutting out of the water are part of the headland of this peninsula, in low tide they are connected by land to where I took this photo.

As you can see from the high water mark which is only slightly exposed on the rock faces, it is high tide now. You can also see from the wake (turbulence), the tide is receding, out toward the ocean to the left. Interested in the height and speed of incoming tide?

More information about the highest tides in the world:
<https://www.bayoffundy.com/about/highest-tides> and
<https://parks.canada.ca/pn-np/nb/fundy/nature/environment/marees-tides>

Mother Nature

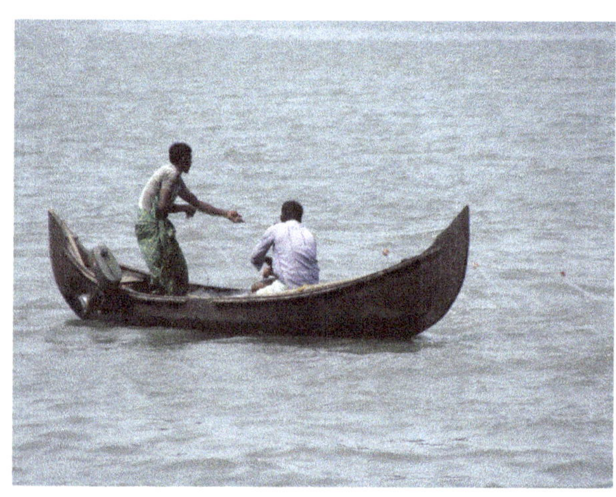

Blessed are those healthy
Cultivating earth daily
At nature's mercy

Photo taken in 2013

Location: Kochi, India

He's got a boat to maintain,

a net to mend,

a skill to hone,

a patience to endure,

and probably a mouth or two to feed.

Murphy's Law Blessing

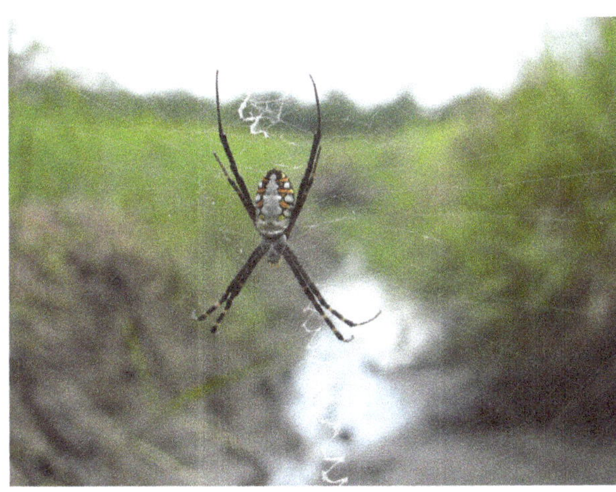

If there are three ways
Left way, right way, and your way
It's the other way

Photo taken in 2010

Location: Phong Dien, Can Tho, Vietnam

Instead of buying the Mekong River ride that my guest house offered, I ventured to the riverbank to negotiate with a boatman for better deal.

A boatwoman approached to tell him off. He complied without a fuss; acknowledging her authority.

The woman offered me her boat ride, same price as the guest house's.

In solidarity for the kind looking boatman, I opted to go back for my guest house's offer.

The next morning my boat waited at the pier. Her again. The same boat woman now had me in her boat.

There was no escape, acknowledging her authority, into the Mekong Delta for village sojourns.

She saw something and took my camera, returned with this shot.

My Kind of Car

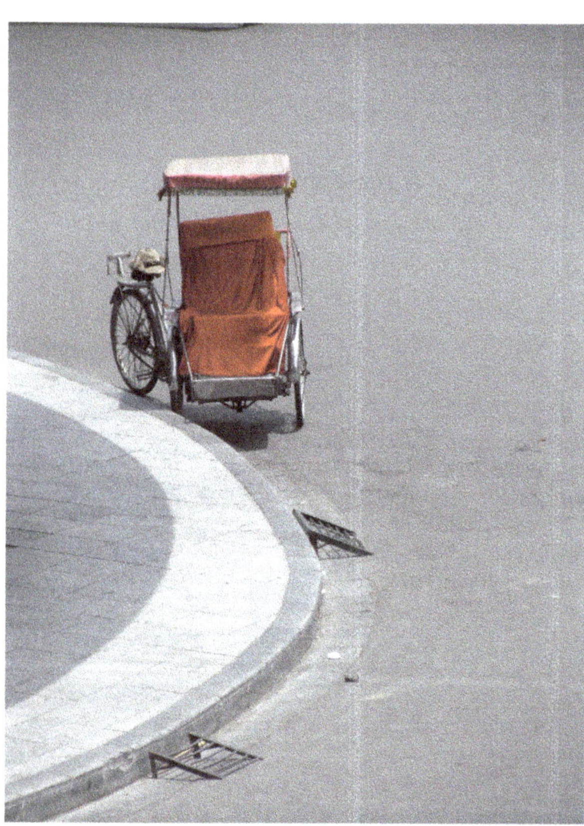

Kick start needs no key
No license nor service fee
It sure is smoke free

Photo taken in 2010

Location: Hanoi, Vietnam

I did not expect a minimalist approach to taking a photo in the middle of a capital city, but here's one.

More information about minimalist photography:

https://iceland-photo-tours.com/articles/photography-tutorials/how-to-make-mesmerising-minimal-photography

Need Two

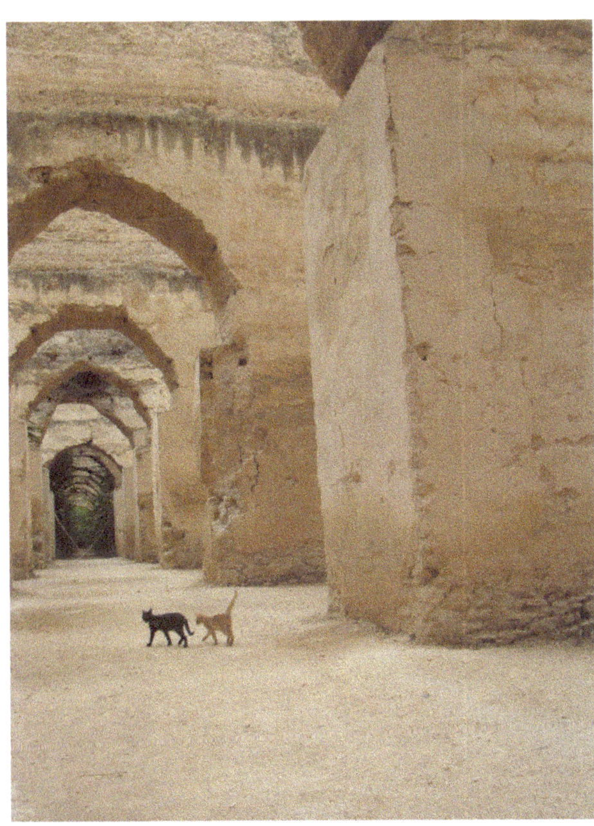

Blue trouser looks good
With a matching shoe to suit
Wear sunglass you should

Photo taken in 2018

Location: Heri es-Souani, Meknes, Morocco

If you like cats, this is the place.

Neighbourhood Clan

Going with no plan
Ran into neighbourhood clan
Good to understand

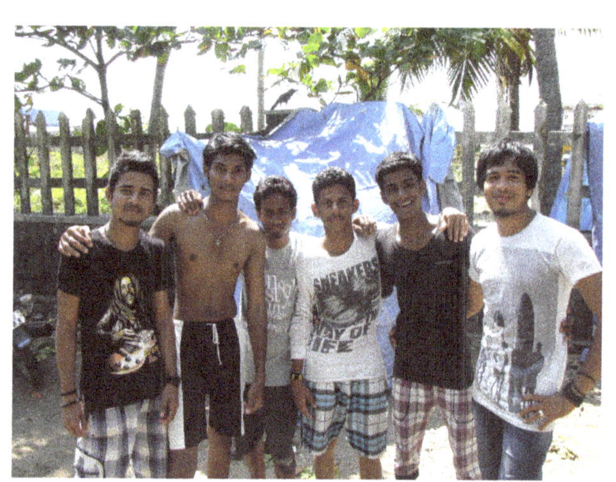

Photo taken in 2013

Location: Vypīn Island, India

Being called uncle is a good feeling indeed.

Neighbourhood Gadgets

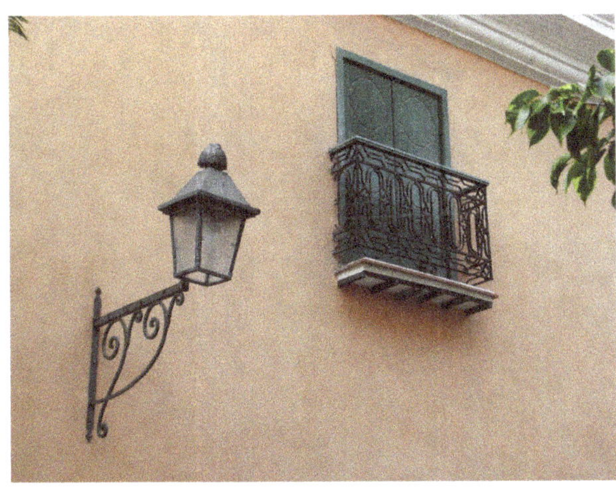

Window of the soul
Once it opens up in whole
A story unfold

Photo taken in 2010

Location: Havana, Cuba

Would you agree that this window, not the size of a door, looks like a balcony door?

Hence, from optical illusion, the building looks higher?

Do you think the size of the lamp tries to validate it?

Or the cleverly scaled "guardrail" does the trick?

Ambiguity can be intriguing.

Nice Music

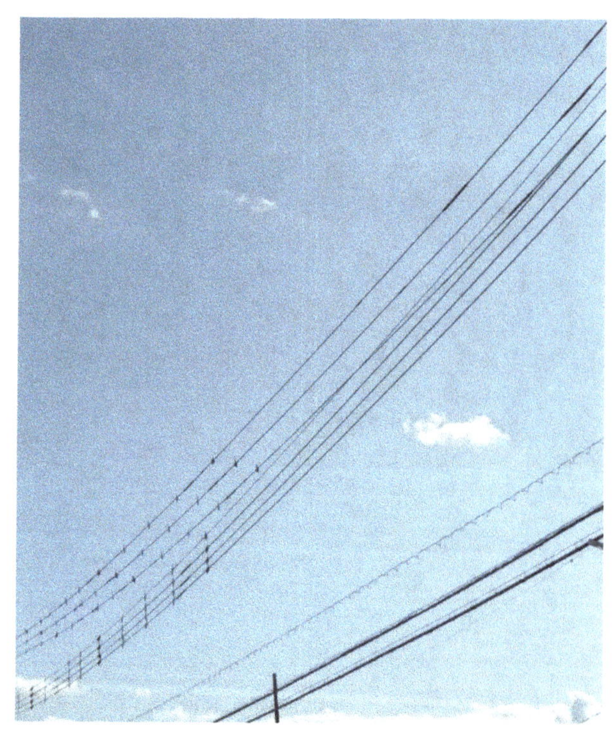

This can't be the staves
On bars no measure engraved
Clef skipped an octave

(Inspired by the Japanese wabi-sabi approach to aesthetics)

Photo taken in 2020

Location: Utsunomiya, Japan

I went back at dusk, when the sky is amber,

hoping to "sight read" the same note in different tone,

got lost, gave up, and settled with this one.

Nook in a Niche

Dark cobbled alley
There hides an age-old beauty
Weathered yet sturdy

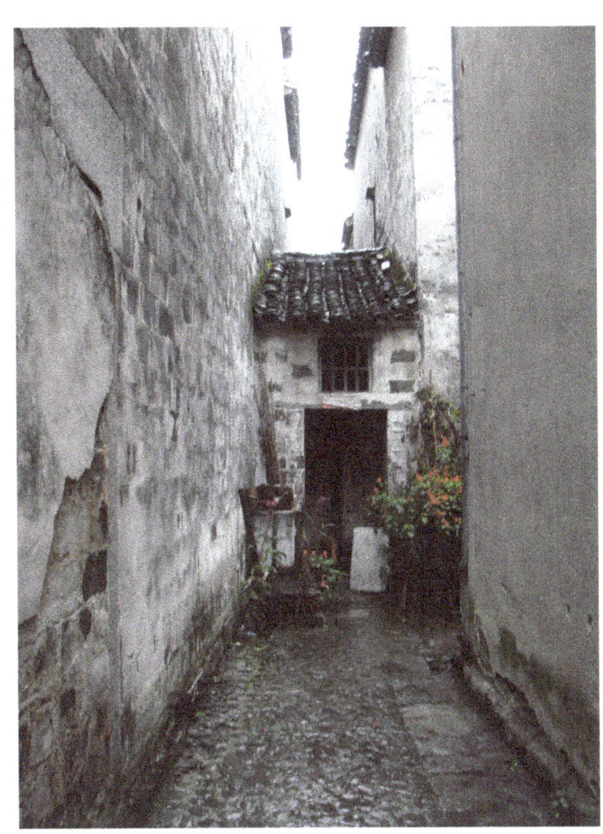

Photo taken in 2008

Location: Hongcun, China

Getting lost in such a maze, amazing!

Old Charm

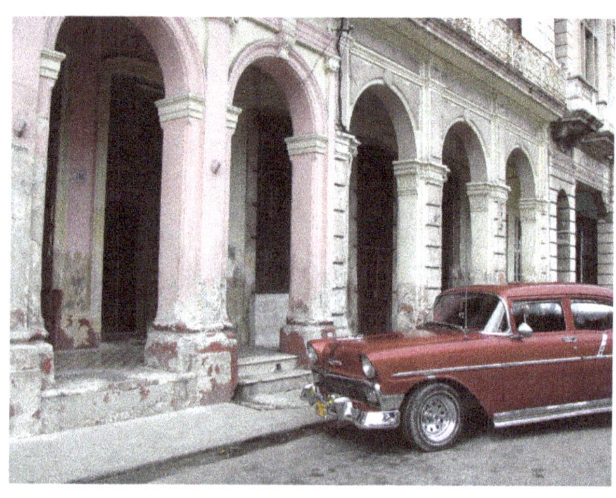

Good old novelty
While modern left abruptly
Endured history

Photo taken in 2010

Location: Havana, Cuba

What is timeless beauty? Does it have to be old?

As Oscar Wilde put it, "It is only the modern that ever becomes old-fashioned."

Once in a Blue Moon

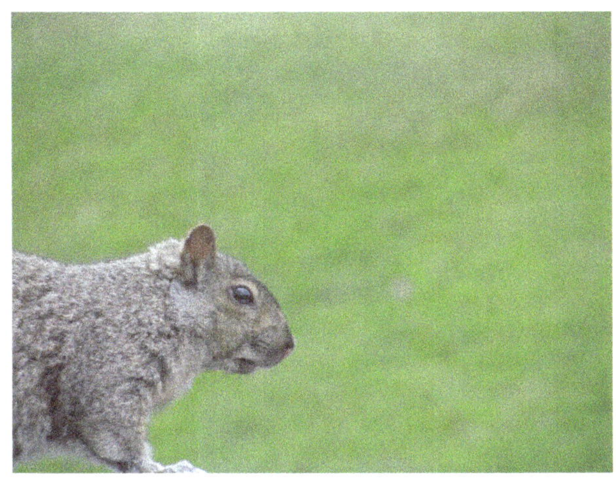

Champion in jumping
Tree to tree perfect landing
Sometimes mishandling

(Inspired by the Indonesian proverb about no one is without flaw)

Photo taken in 2010

Location: Montreal, Canada

This squirrel came for a nut or two.

I didn't have any to spare, took his photo instead.

If a squirrel misplaces a nut, it will turn into a full grown oak?

Once Upon a Time

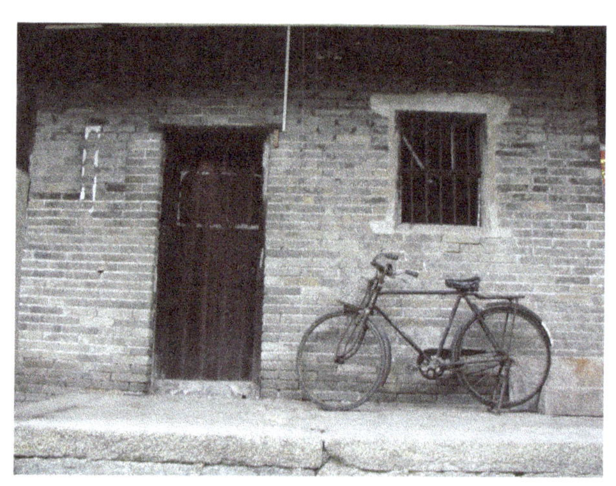

A clan in oldtown
A village once a hometown
Have they gone downtown

Photo taken in 2012

Location: Tai'an Lou, Dapu, China

Sometimes memories are all that hold people together.

One Day

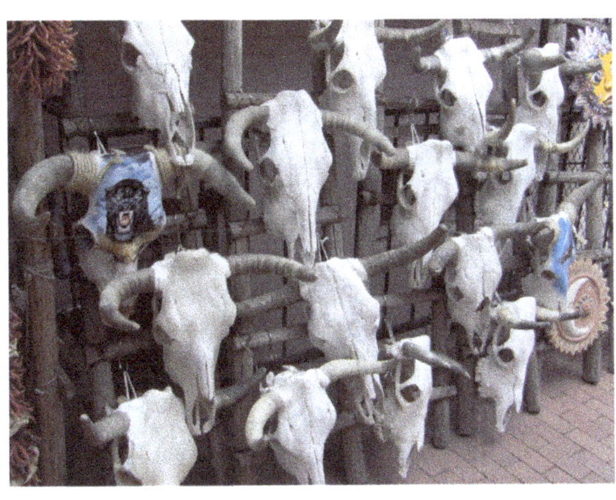

Inevitably
And indiscriminately
Part of a journey

Photo taken in 2007

Location: Santa Fe, U.S.A.

Bull horns alone have an array of styles.

We then give them adjectives and verbs for description.

Other Coin's Side

Pouring had halted
Fun rides were all suspended
Boatmen have rested

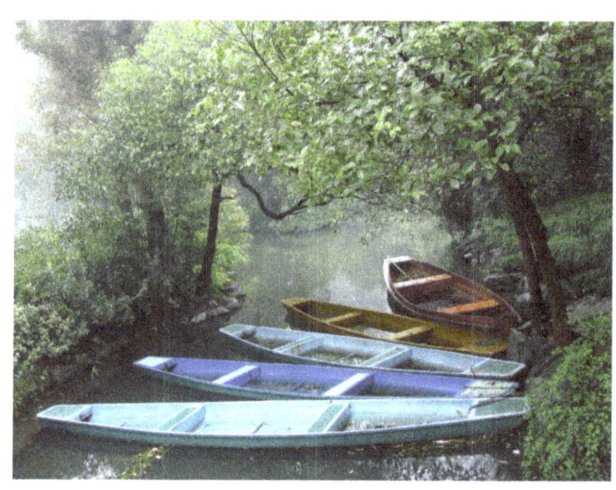

Photo taken in 2008

Location: Hangzhou, China

I took a vertical shot, but the skylight entered my camera, which caused competing exposures: the bright sky rendered the boats in the shade under exposed. To compensate for brighter exposure I aimed at the shaded boats, which made the sky too bright, hence causing the skylight to "bleed" into the leaves. I opted for horizontal shot, without the sky.

More information about exposure in photography:
<https://photographylife.com/what-is-exposure>

Palette

Strumming from next door
In wee hours upstairs snore
Babies protest more

And the alleys howl
No soul dares to call it foul
Endures the night owl

Photo taken in 2008

Location: Halifax, Canada

Many houses in Halifax are old buildings, preserved for their historical, architectural, and aesthetic values. I tried to maximize the horizontal coverage of this row of colourful façades into the frame, if the street had been wide enough for me to step back further, I would have had taken a panoramic view. It turns out that this angle offers a fresh composition.

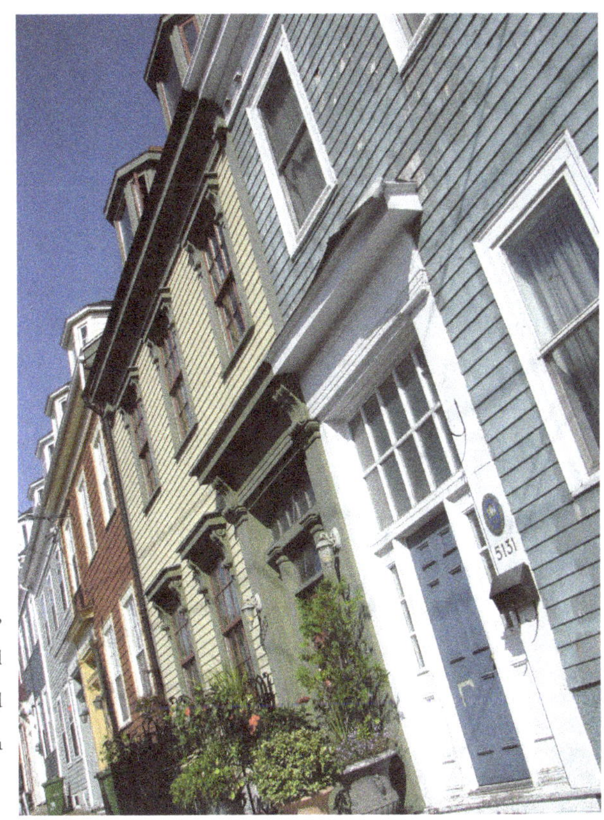

Palindrome

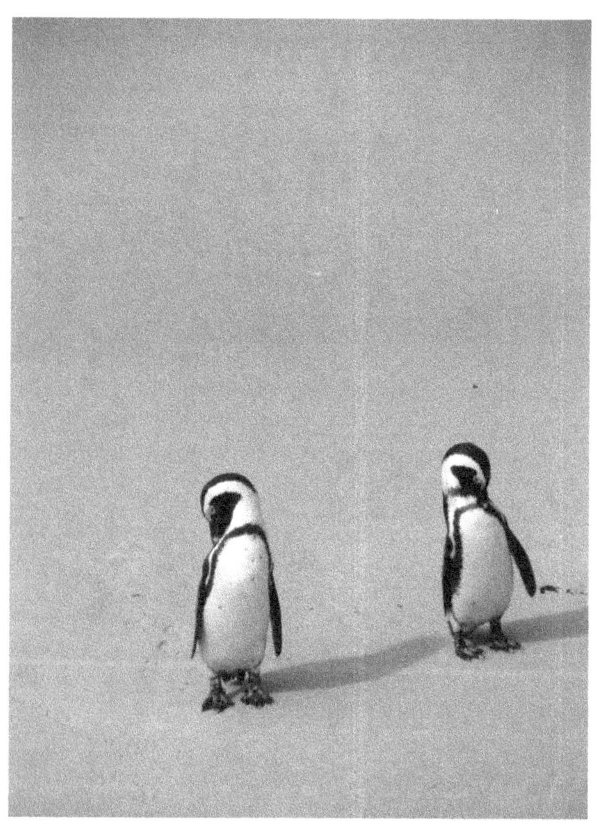

In tango we hold
And sweep the floor with the toe
Swing her to-and-fro

Photo taken in 2018

Location: False Bay, South Africa

Oblivious to human's presence, coming ashore, waddling flat footed

straight toward the camera and posed this "mirrored" duet.

Patiently

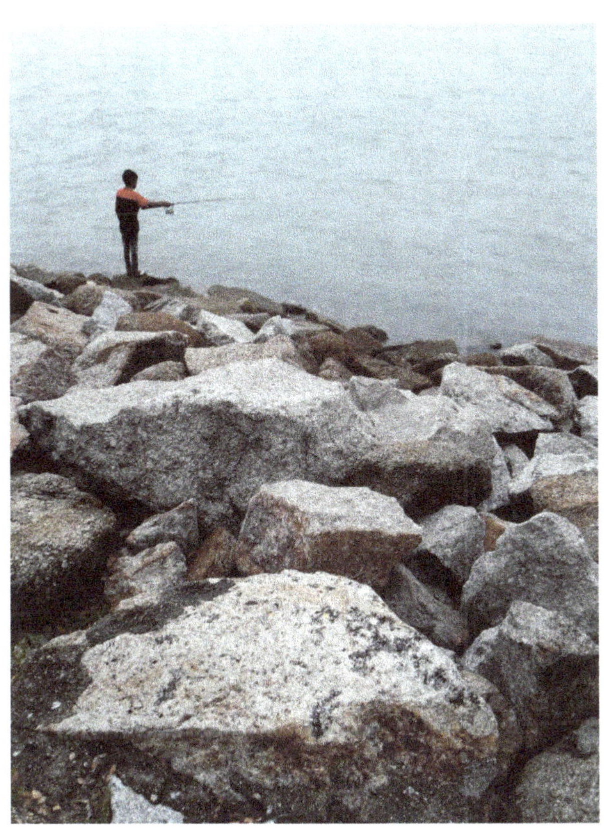

Despite getting late
For something to take the bait
Patiently he waits

Photo taken in 2019

Location: Penang, Malaysia

Patience is virtue.

Pattern

For consistency
Pattern is a quality
Always trustworthy

Photo taken in 2020

Location: Hachimanyama Koen, Utsunomiya, Japan

This is *hanami* (*hana*=flower, *mi*=beautiful) season, when the *sakura* blossoms everywhere. The weather can still be cold, some shrubs are not ready to come out, leaving their manicured form bare; by late spring, all of them would wear verdant.

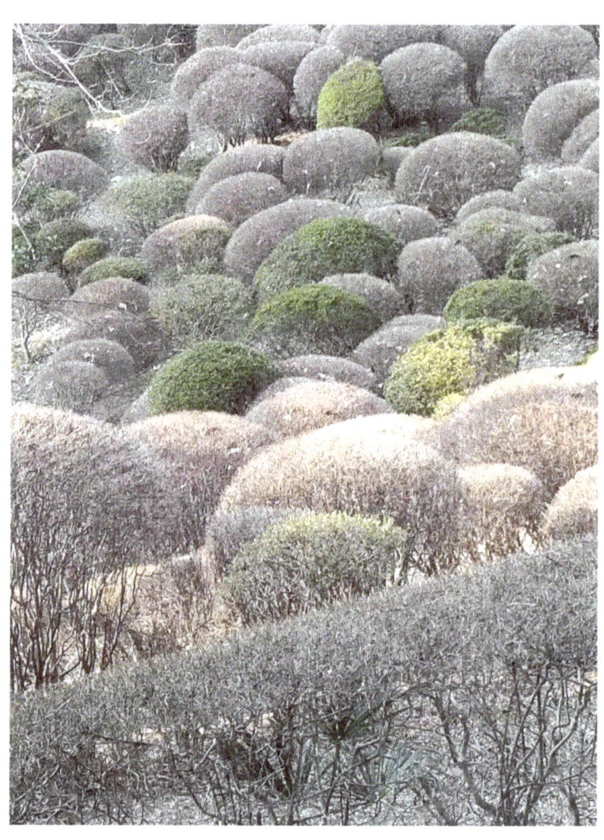

Perspective 101

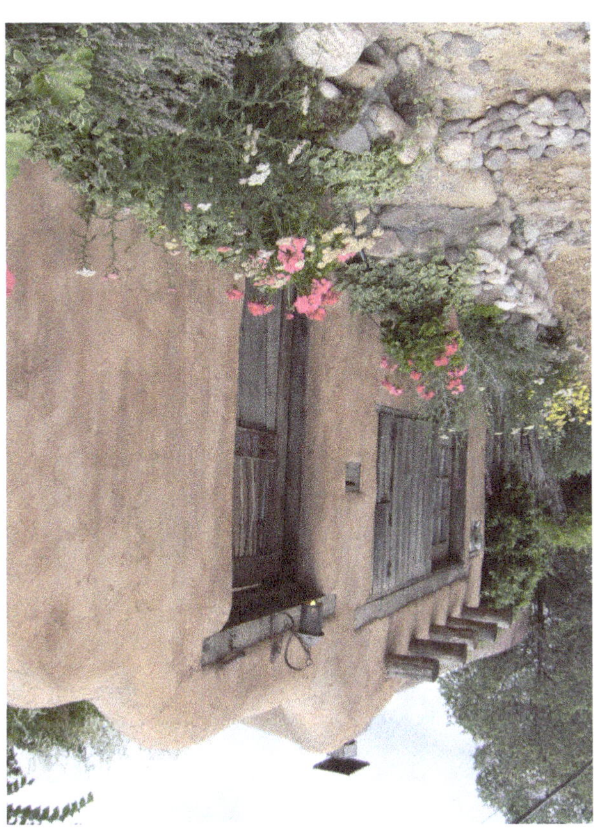

Interpretations
A subject of contentions
Invoke reactions

From one perspective
Subjective or objective
Is interpretive

Photo taken in 2007

Location: Santa Fe, New Mexico, U.S.A.

The "free flowing" feel of this adobe (Pueblo style) home fascinates me.

All lines are loose, as if they were drawn by a nervous old hand.

I find that by looking at it upside down, it accentuates such attribute,

and puts the expected norm out of context; offering a different perspective.

Pinnacle

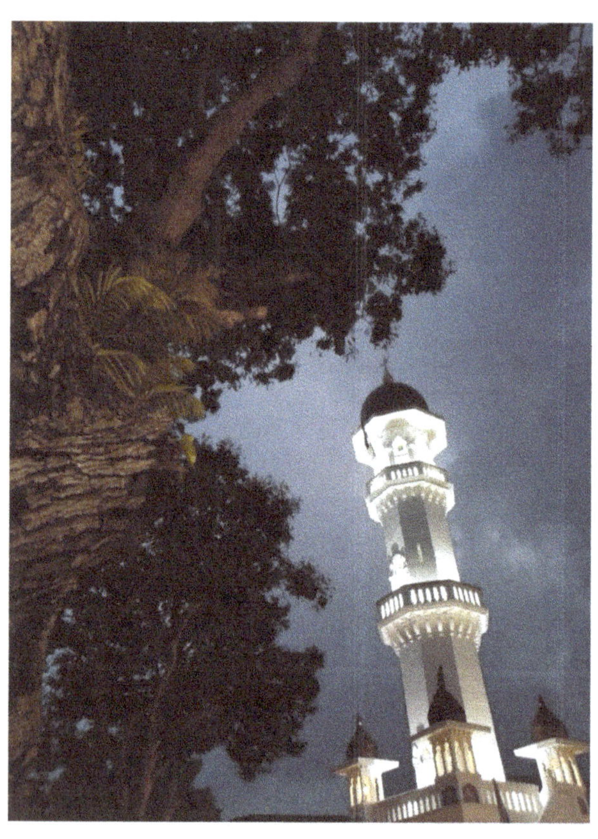

Glancing up at dusk
A slender glows in the dark
From ground it embarks

Photo taken in 2019

Location: Masjid Kapitan Keling, Penang, Malaysia

During the day, it's a different scene when the light comes from above.

The ambience glows after dark. Lighting dictates photo composition.

Poetic Space

Diminishing depth
Echoes along rhythmic path
Must be good at math

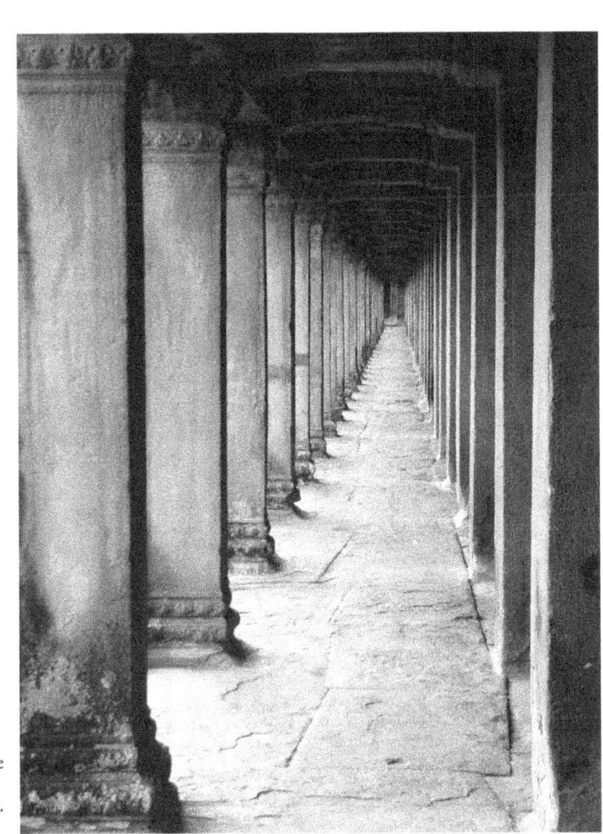

Photo taken in 2010

Location: Angkor Wat, near Siem Reap, Cambodia

Leaving my guesthouse before dawn on a motorbike, riding in the dark, hoping to see sunrise onsite. The sun must have risen on the wrong side that morning; I didn't get what I had imagined, columns with shadows. Somehow, this shot is one of my favourites.

Purification

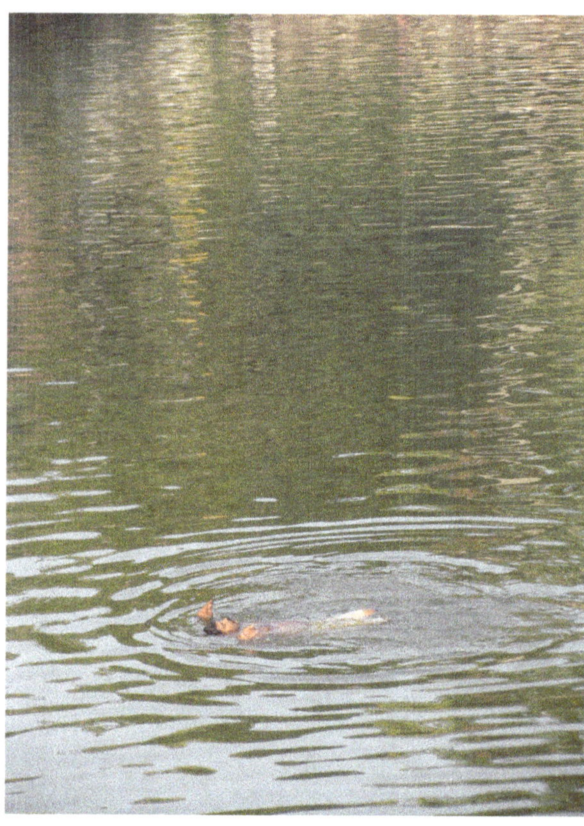

From lake to river
Possessing healing power
A purifier

Photo taken in 2013

Location: Varkala, India

This is a reservoir beside a temple, locals use it for bathing. This man, buoyant in his own world, seems to enjoy a treat of blissful cleansing. You can tell from the reflection of the water that the surrounding is colourful.

Rhetorically Speaking

One gaze to the left
In fact both gaze to the left
Just one to your left

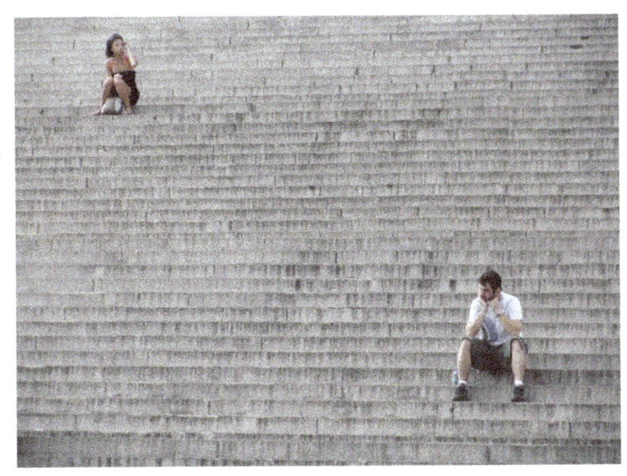

Photo taken in 2010

Location: Havana, Cuba

I have a confession to make,

I removed two other people from this photo.

Rhythm from the Field

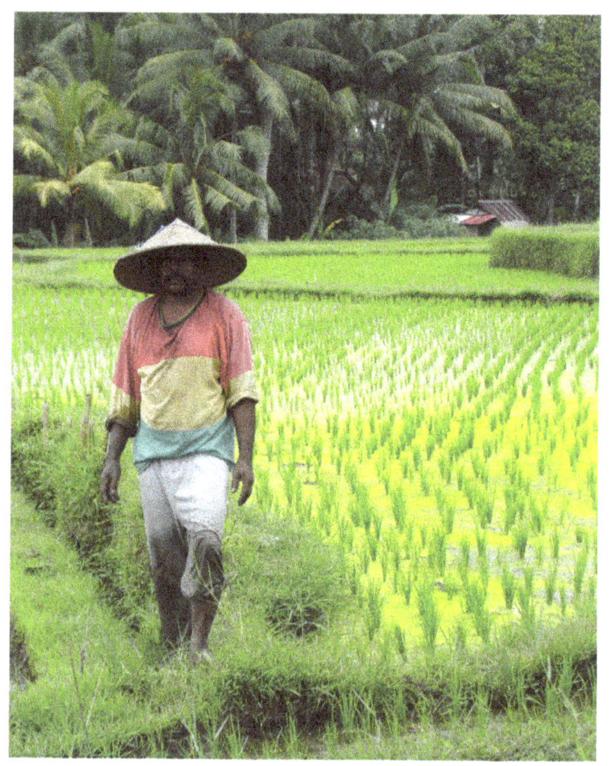

Toil for seeds to grow
Submerge low not overflow
Grains of tomorrow

Photo taken in 2017

Location: Ubud, Indonesia

Pak petani came to greet from his well-taken-care-of verdant *sawah*. *Pak* means father in Indonesian, a polite title used for addressing a male adult person of any age. *Petani* means farmer. *Sawah*, as you may have guessed from the context, means rice field.

Ribbit Ribbit

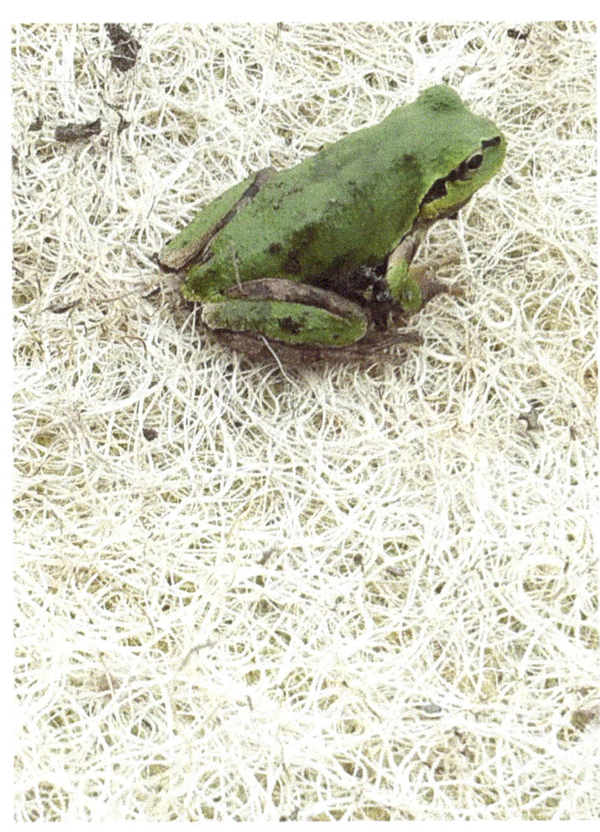

One ribbit pipes out
Distant chorus chants about
Crescendo throughout

Photo taken in 2020

Location: Utsunomiya, Japan

They may be just the size of a finger nail,

their calls can be heard throughout the neighborhood.

Frogs, or *kaeru* in Japanese, symbolize good luck,

the same pronunciation for returning home (safely.)

Rite of Passage

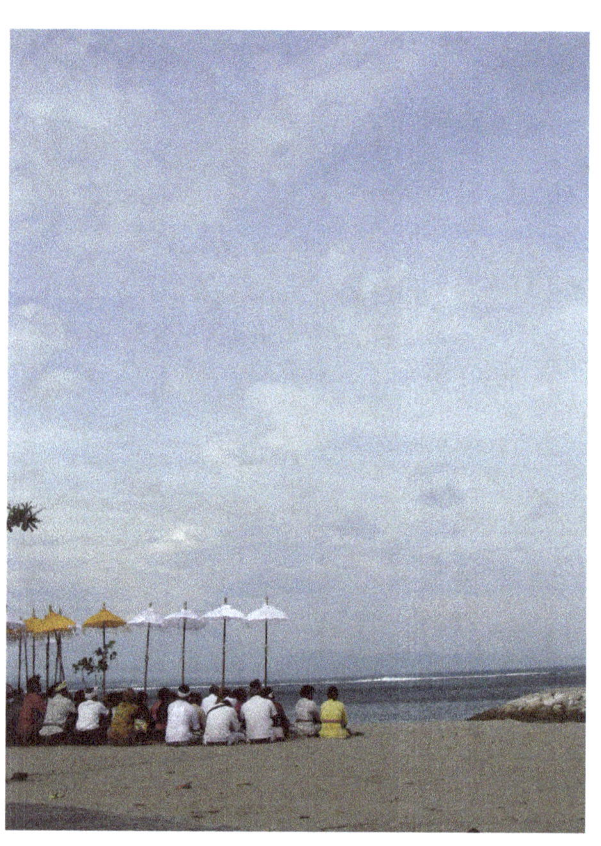

To see someone off
To the horizon far off
The soul taken off

Photo taken in 2012

Location: Sanur, Indonesia

No one spoke in this funeral.

Together in silence...dignified.

Running Errands

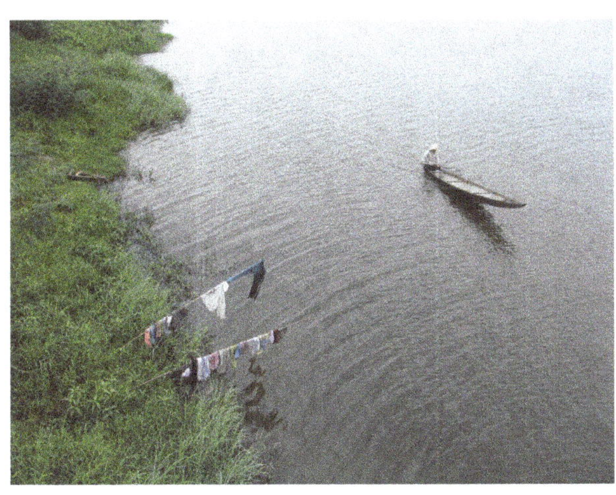

Kitchen needs sugar
Panic stumbling departure
Urgent as ever

Kitchen now needs salt
As soon as sugar's been brought
Of course it's my fault

Photo taken in 2010

Location: Hue, Vietnam

A light boat has high buoyancy and less stable,

but it offers speed since the hull sits higher in the water and hence

requires less force to push less amount of water out of the way.

Because it is light, the bow rides high off the water,

which reduces the water resistance on its hull.

Sea of Fog

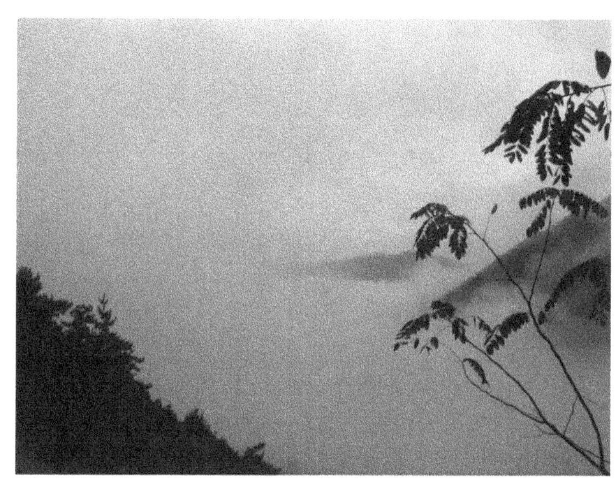

When days are gloomy
Silver lining unlikely
One must find beauty

Photo taken in 2008

Location: Huangshan, China

Clearing only intermittently, the fog was persistent,

my glasses got foggy, so was my camera lens.

My shirt was wet, from sweating while climbing up here.

This scene lasted only seconds as the fog was constantly on the move.

Seasonal Hue

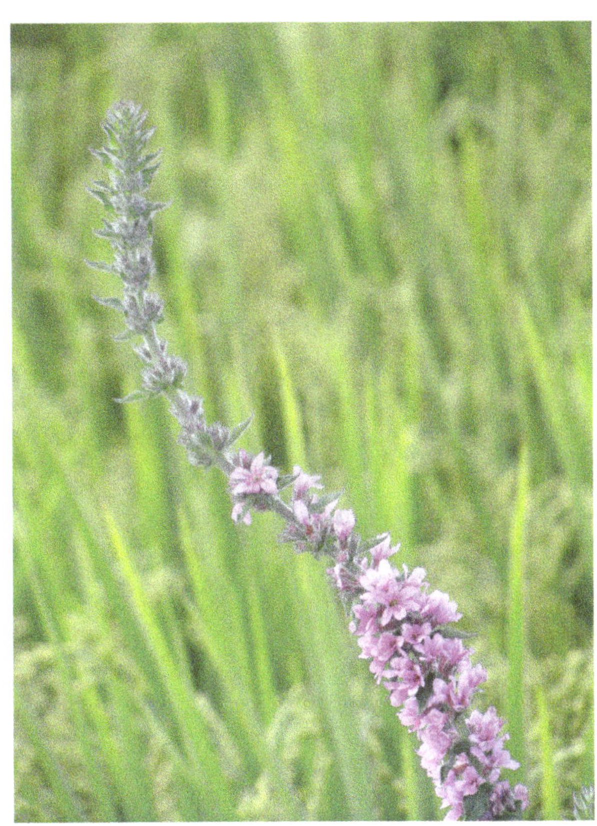

They all come and go
From high mountains to meadows
Next spring foreshadows

Photo taken in 2018

Location: Dali, China

I was going to rent a Harley; never ridden one.

I changed my mind; too dear. I walked instead.

Had I gone ahead for the bike,

I wouldn't have met this beauty in the middle of the rice fields.

Self Reflection

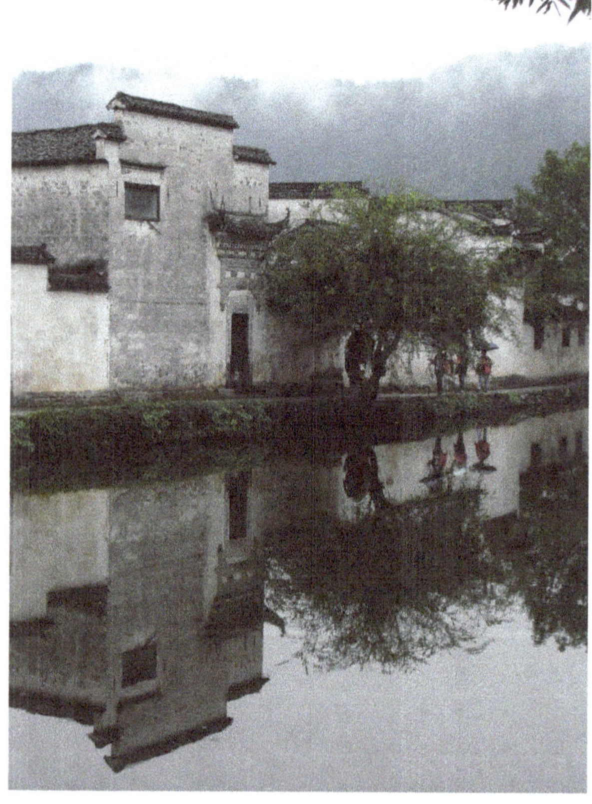

To see my own deed
Without a mirror I need
A self-reflection indeed

Photo taken in 2008

Location: Hongcun Ancient Village, China

Despite the spitty rain, the surface was flat as a mirror.

Despite the weather, it was a blessing in disguise; less tourists.

Sequence of Events

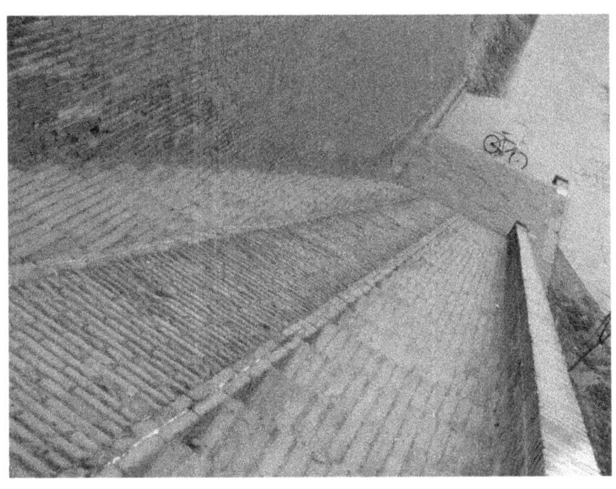

Yesterday's reclaimed
Whatever today proclaims
Tomorrow shall claim

Photo taken in 2012

Location: Pingyao, China

In meeting a distant high point, one must aim higher to compensate for the gravity like a released arrow.

Silhouette

At the end of day
The sun has set at the bay
Night owls out to play

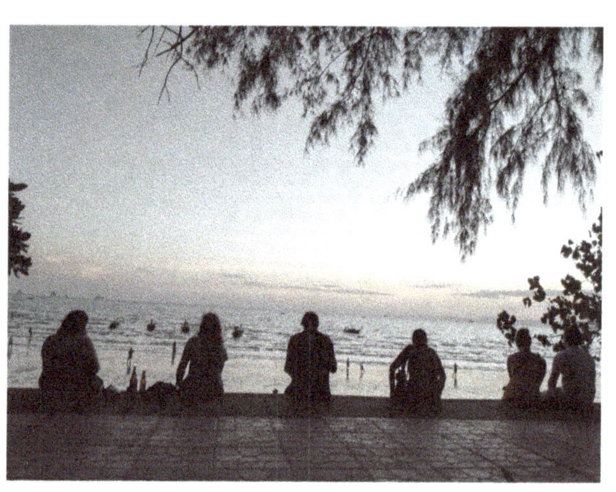

Photo taken in 2020

Location: Ao Nang, Thailand

Just profiles against the twilight.

Solitaire

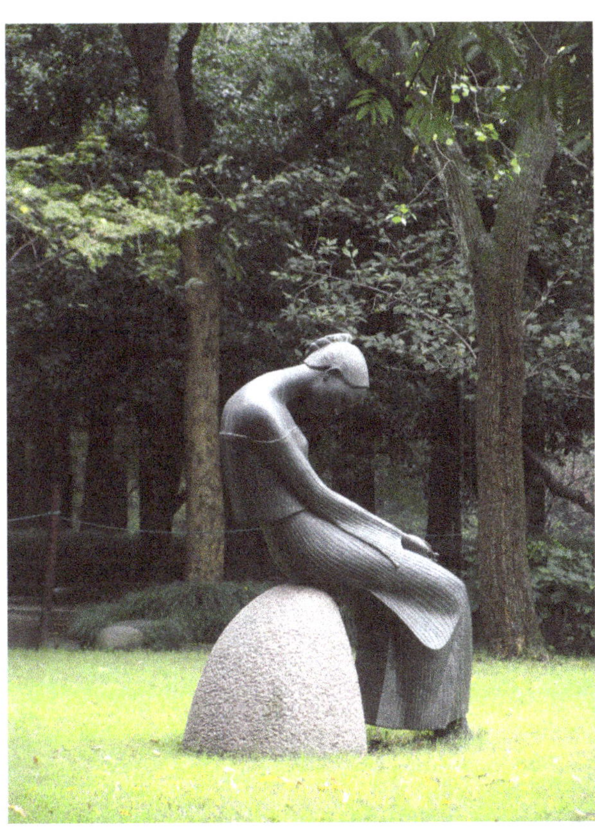

Rustling on tree top
Lean on to where one shall drop
Counting the tears drop

(Inspired by the proverb:

Smile and the world smiles with you,

cry and you cry alone.)

Photo taken in 2008

Location: Hangzhou, China

In getting lost, one finds the unexpected.

Confucius said that roads were made for journeys, not destination.

Stressful Beauty

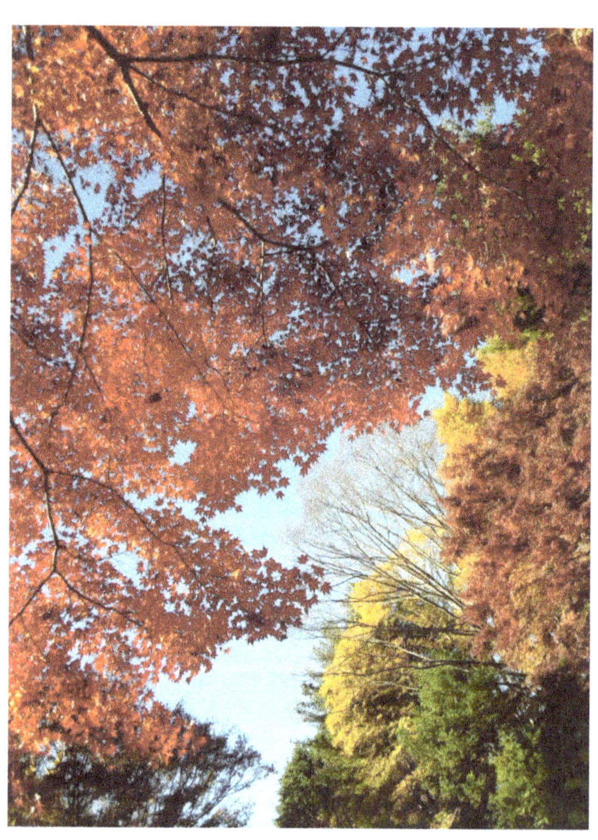

Before foliage fall
Illuminating for all
Frozen they stand tall

Photo taken in 2020

Location: Utsunomiya, Japan

Autumn hues, from yellow to brown, they are all here.

Subjectivity

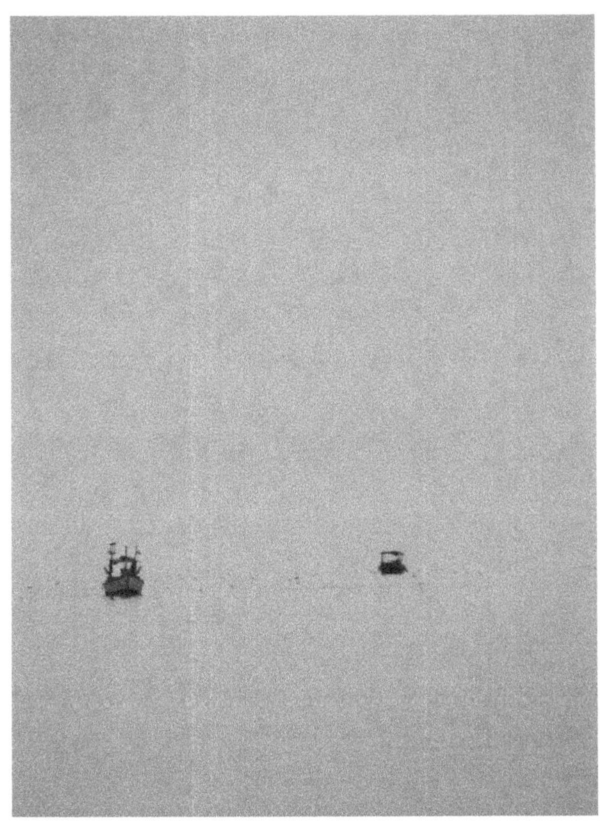

When earth and sky merge
Where horizon sees no surge
Submerge or emerge

Photo taken in 2010

Location: Nha Trang, Vietnam

Ten times zoom without a tripod. Apologies for the shaky hand.

Tale of a Herd

Once upon a time
When headwind and tailwind rhymed
All the moos stood fine

Pasture our lifeline
So long as the sun will shine
Our turf is defined

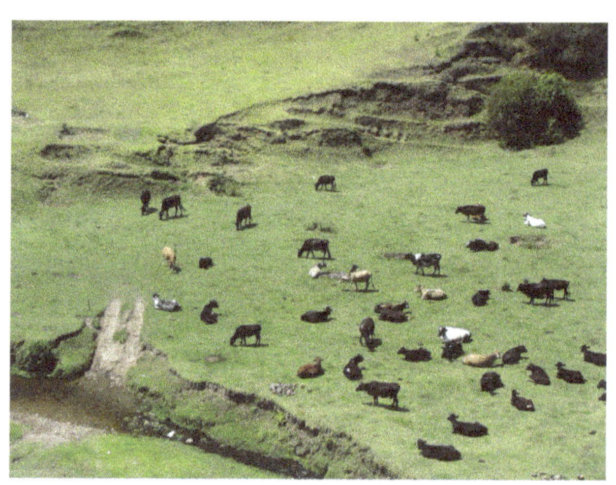

Photo taken in 2013

Location: Somewhere in the mountains near Munar, India

At the bottom right, notice the cattle laying down are facing in the same direction.

At the bottom left, notice the uphill track from the river, what a joy ride.

Terrace Symphony

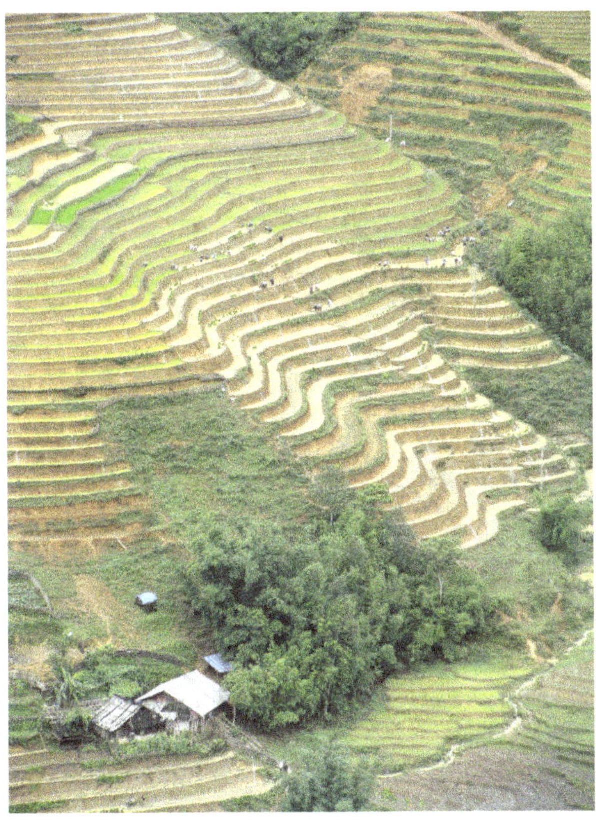

Verdant vows to play
Bowing to the breeze they sway
Golden the next day

Photo taken in 2010

Location: Sapa, Vietnam

Imagine this being a stairs, where risers' height and treads' depth are almost equal from top to bottom; indicating a steady climb of the 45° slope. Being communal is key to an agrarian civilization.

Texture

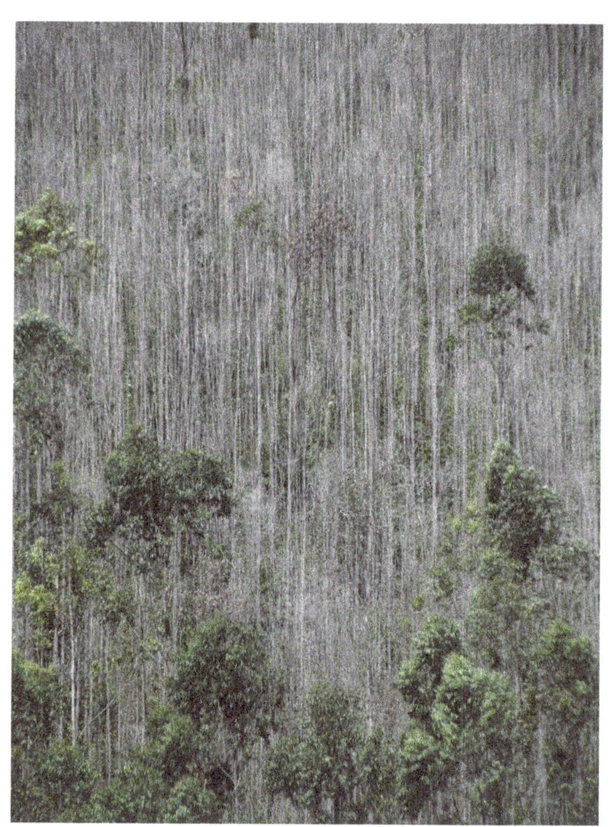

Verticality
Forming the majority
Almost unearthly

Photo taken in 2013

Location: Somewhere near Bison Valley, Kerala, India

What prompted this slope to have such texture?

Clearly stress for the trees, but beauty to other species.

The Child in Us

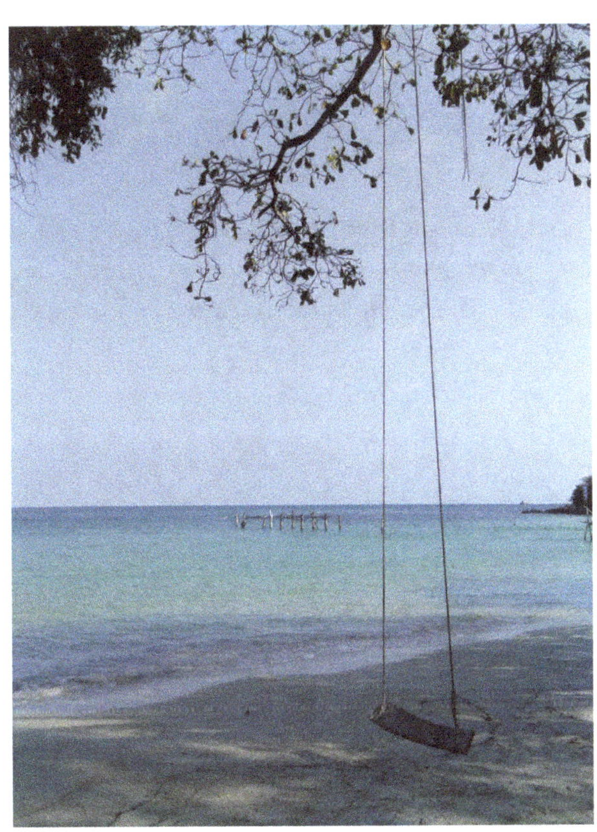

Giggling little stubs
Who just refuse to grow up
Happy with hiccups

Photo taken in 2019
Location: Koh Samet, Thailand

I searched online for the synonym of swing, fifty of
them came back in verbs and nouns.

The Duel

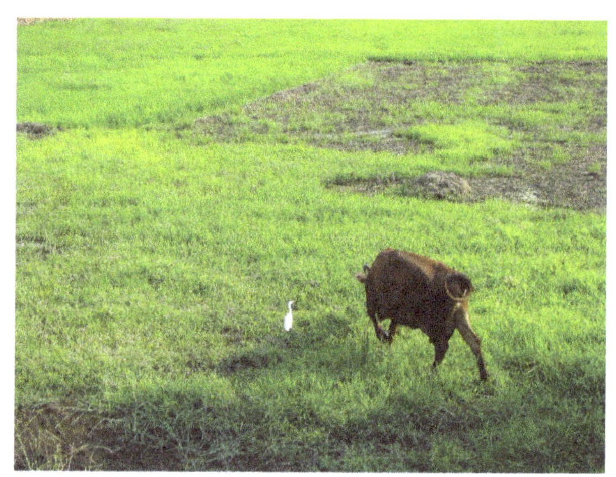

Here comes raging charge
Here goes frightened sideway barge
Settling who's in charge

Photo taken in 2013

Location: Kollam, India

That bird has got to be really annoying.

That cow has got to be really hot blooded.

The Shaded Face

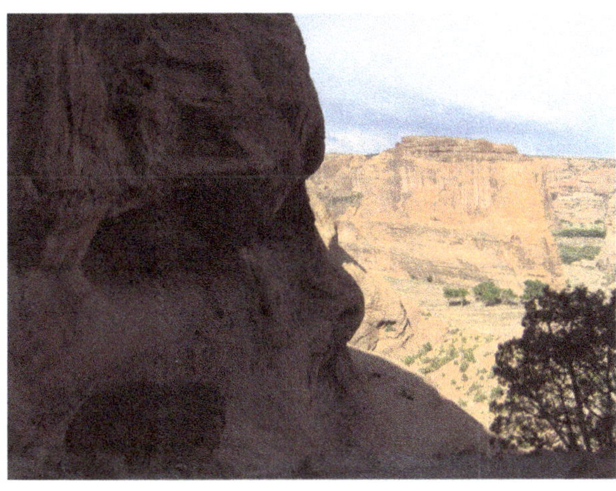

In search of true self
One must confront his dark side
The side he must hide

Photo taken in 2007

Location: Somewhere in Arizona, U.S.A.

There was utter silence in these canyons, you can hear the feathers of birds slicing through the air. Out of sight, a thundering gallop down below was crispy and amplified; so loud as if it was within reach. On the way down, clinging to the cliff, I was greeted by an elderly aboriginal woman, who was on the way back from tending her sick goat, every day; slowly and dignified.

The Time is Now

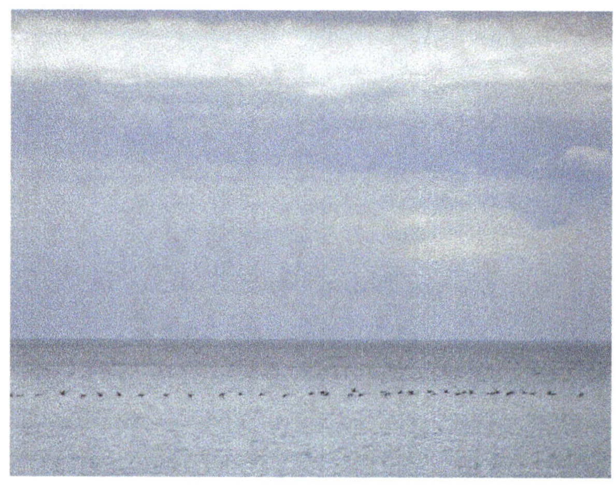

Natural leader
Seen and proven since youngster
Across vast water

Photo taken in 2010

Location: Lake Ontario, Canada

More information about Canada geese migration:

<https://www.canada.ca/en/environment-climate-change/services/

migratory-bird-conservation/managing-conflicts/frequently-asked-questions.html>

Tight-knit

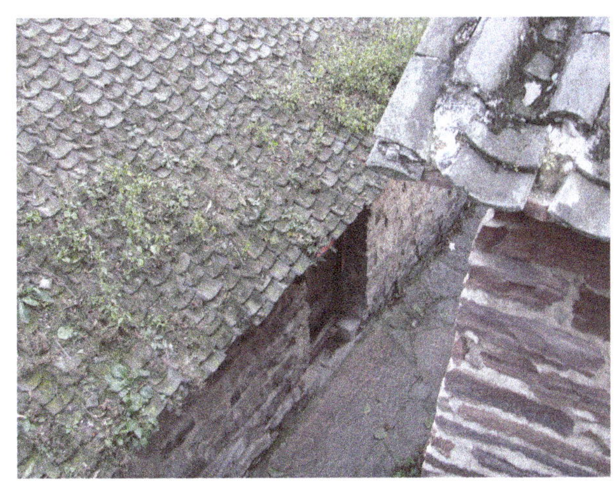

Everyone knows you
Even the squirrel's nephew
Smelling neighbour's stew

Photo taken in 2008

Location: Guoliangcun, China

This ancient stone hamlet perched on a cliff, naturally the topography is steep.

I took the picture of this alley below from another alley above it, almost perpendicularly.

Can you visualize the "vanishing" point of lines converging toward the top right corner?

Timing

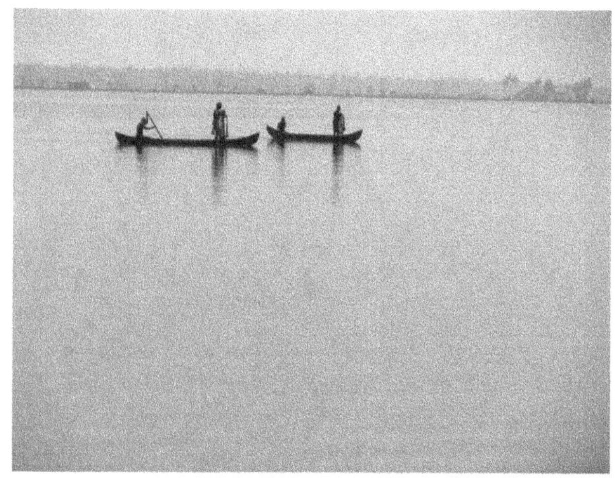

Fishing and patience
When to cast the nets at once
Forward in silence

Photo taken in 2013

Location: Vypīn Island, India

Wisdom is nature's gift, it comes from knowing what is not spoken.

Trash & Treasure

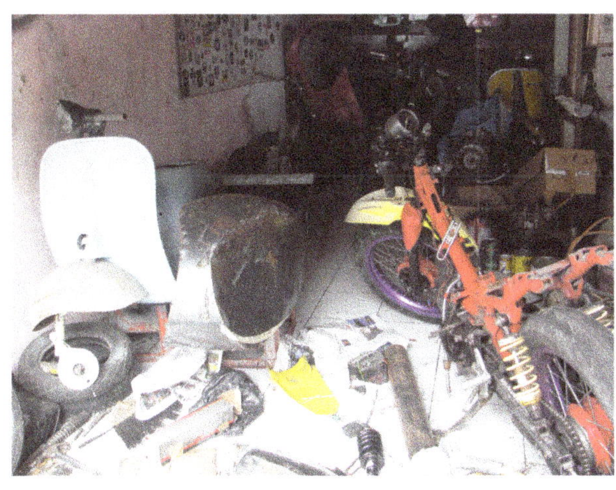

Rotten scooter yay
Everything dismantled yay
Your trash my gem yay

Photo taken in 2012

Location: Ubud, Indonesia

As a boy, I used to make my own toys. It was a lot of fun.

Leonardo da Vinci said, "Art is never finished, only abandoned."

Trodden Path

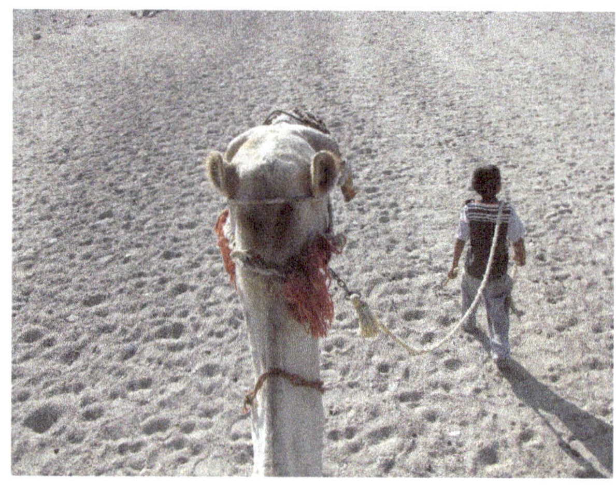

Photo taken in 2016

Location: Sahara Desert, Egypt

The ears tune upward and backward,

toward the sound of the camera being turned on

which is not desert sound.

Precious is water
A hide pouch of thirst quencher
Crucial life saver

When distance is great
Regardless of pace or gait
Surrender to fate

Tugboat

I may be tiny
Giant ships depend on me
To guide them to sea

Photo taken in 2009

Location: Halifax Harbour, Canada

I wanted a portrait of Theodore, that means no background distraction, just like a passport photo. I knew his route, but not his schedule. To take this picture, I waited on Halifax old bridge with my camera over the ledge. Security was quick to dispatch. In a golf cart an officer approached to inquire if I was okay. After explaining my admiration for my city's icon I got permission to have my wish granted with a promise not to climb up anything on the bridge. Theo came back. He was a hard working tugboat.

To see a bird's eye view video of Theodore in Halifax Harbour:

<https://theodoretugboat.ca/>

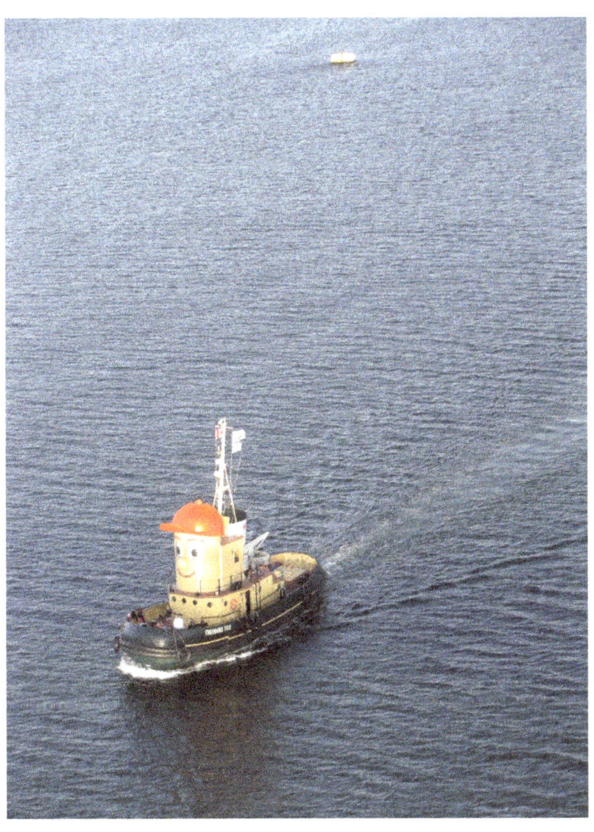

Tunnel Vision

As all else are shunned
Decisions are made and done
One sees only one

Photo taken in 2017

Location: Zadar, Croatia

Charles Barkley said that sometimes that light at the end of the tunnel is a train. I was not comfortable waiting in this dark tunnel, but it paid off: a boldly framed silhouette in motion.

Two Lamps and a Shadow

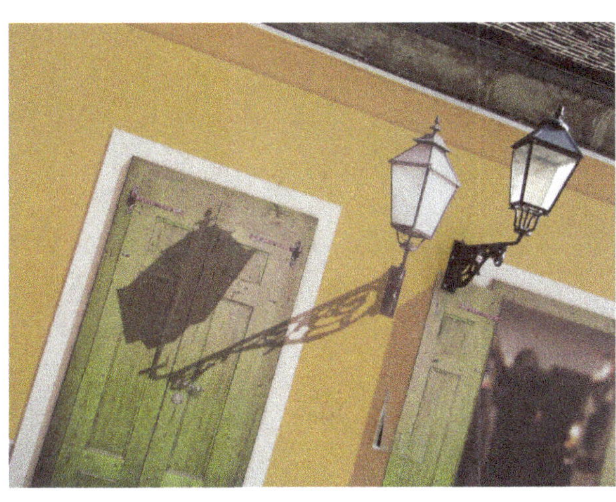

While displays wrestle
From factual to fictional
No twos are equal

One is functional
If not psychological
One is a mural

Photo taken in 2017

Location: Zagreb, Croatia

The doors are a mural. So is the lamp with shadow.

Ultimate Window

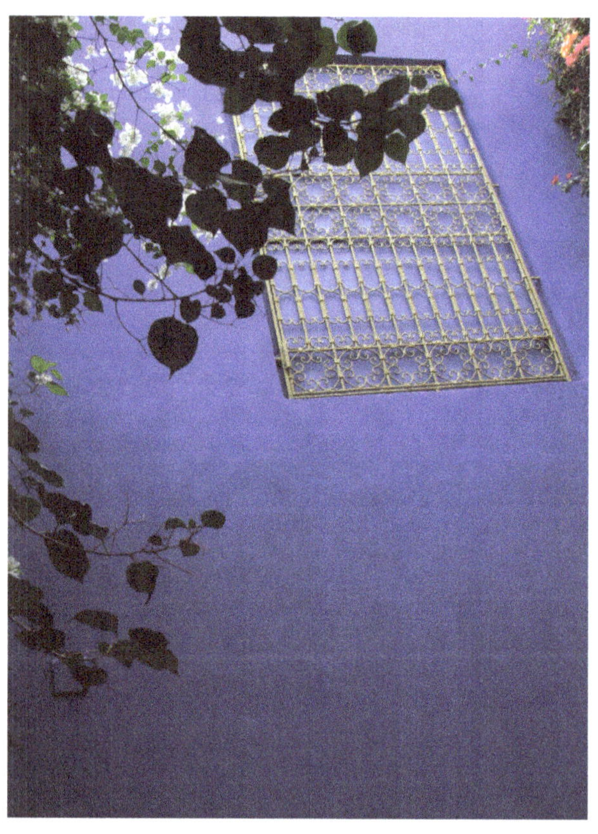

Framed high in layout
No light nor sound in or out
Forever shutout

Photo taken in 2018

Location: Jardin Majorelle, Marrakech, Morocco

Without such uniqueness---would it change the plot?

Uncertainty

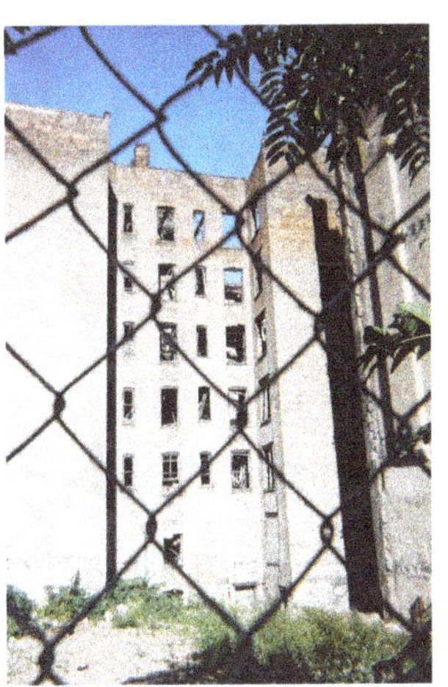

What tale to be told
Wonder tomorrow be bold
What is there to hold

Photo taken in 1997

Location: Harlem, New York, USA

From this side of the fence one sees neglect.

From that side of the fence one sees neglector.

Unlikely Place

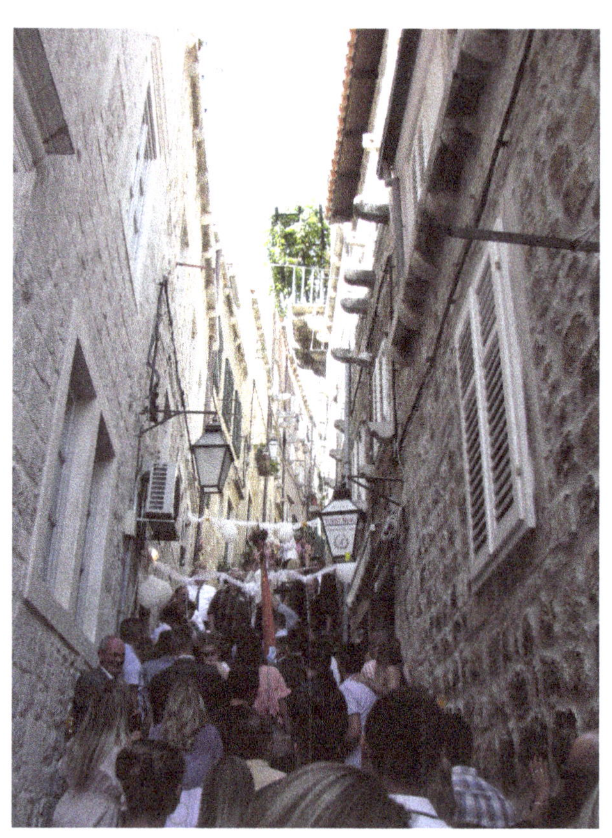

Wedding on the stairs
Not invited I was there
All I see is hair

Photo taken in 2017

Location: Dubrovnik, Croatia

Once up, hard to come down as the crowd wants up.

Unspoken Language

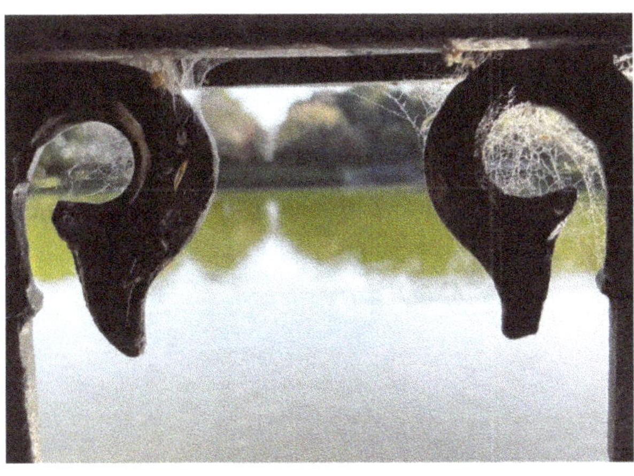

Rhetoric backbone
Body language has its tone
That can stand alone

Photo taken in 2020

Location: Utsunomiya, Japan

This little show was made possible by the sun hanging at certain angle and thanks to the water below for bouncing up the light.

Vernacular Dwellings

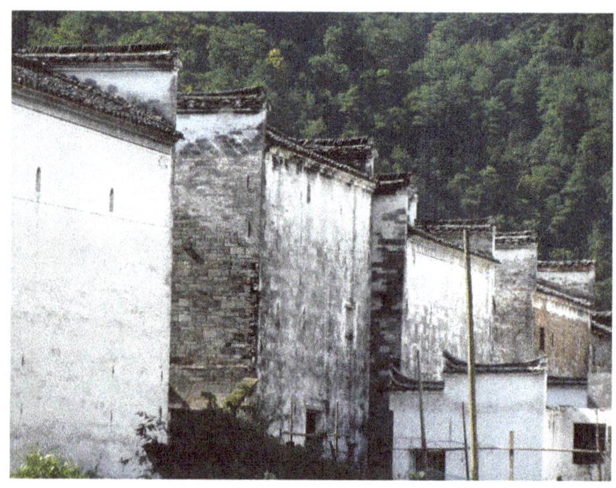

Forego colourful
Of the haves and powerful
Despite successful

Photo taken in 2008

Location: Somewhere in Jiangxi, China

Huizhou architecture, characterized by plain (to discourage attention) high walls (to maximize interior space to store wealth), whitewashed façade (to appear modest), narrow windows placed high above ground (to discourage burglary) for ventilation rather than for aesthetics, black tile roofs (for durability and low maintenance), the signature partition walls always higher than roof ridges (to reduce spread of fire), and the walls are all roofed; for looks.

Vernacular Status

Whitewash walls abound
For modesty to be found
Status all around

Who's who in the hood
One just needs to tilt and look
Details in the mood

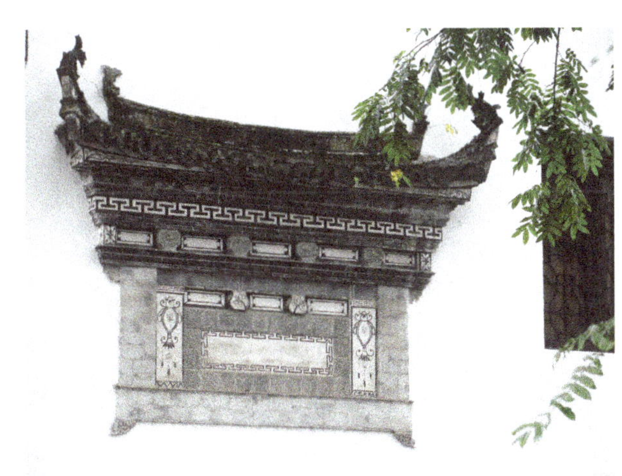

Photo taken in 2008

Location: Hongcun, China

Just a small hamlet surrounded by misty mountains.

Wealth and status can be seen from the façade of the building,

the more elaborated the decoration, the more wealth it implies.

Warning Sign

Horizon's forming
Announced a distant rumbling
Something forthcoming

Photo taken in 2018

Location: Somewhere in South Africa

My poem says something was rumbling.

That is just for the rhyming.

Nothing rumbled nor forthcoming.

Although the mist moved quickly in my direction,

and in no time, the peak seen here disappeared,

totally covered by air moisture.

Weathering Heights

High up the mountain
There rest a wisdom fountain
Where wisdom's written

Photo taken in 2017

Location: Cetina River Valley near Omis, Croatia

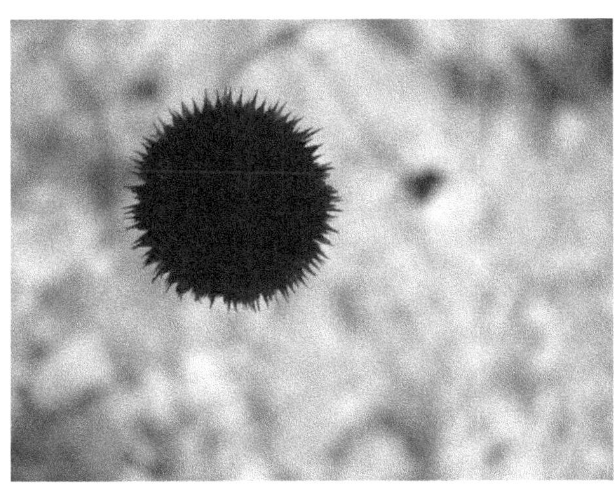

Totally unplanned I took a bus to a seaside town.

Following upstream I was suddenly alone.

The town was no longer in sight.

Only towering cliffs on both sides.

Beautiful in all directions.

Along the valley, crispy cold wind funneled in.

Blowing downstream, it whipped my face.

Plants wiggled in excitement,

refusing to stay still for a pose.

After several attempts,

a top view revealed.

A solo crown on a leafless stem,

braving the relentless draft,

in solitude.

Weaver's hand

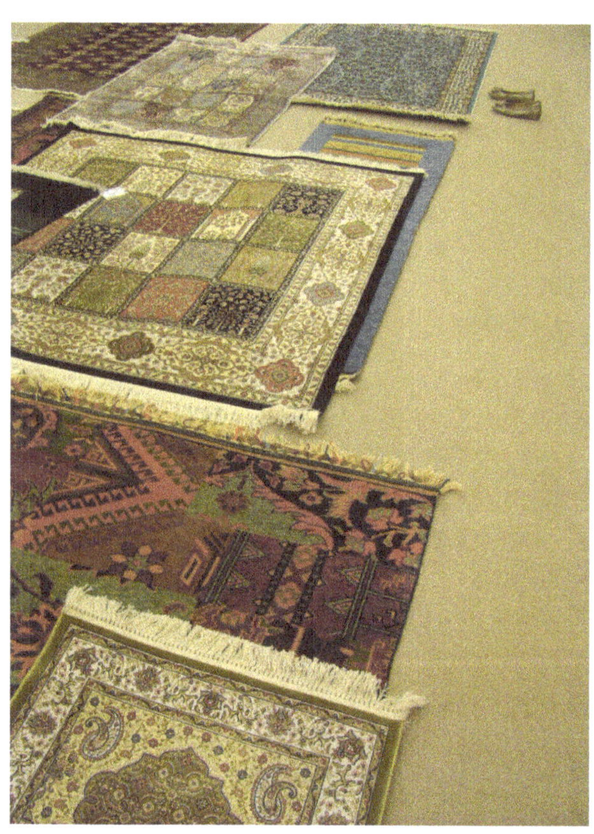

On the loom they merged
Through the warp the weft submerged
There beauty emerged

Photo taken in 2018

Location: Somewhere in Turkey

This was a showroom of a rug factory.

The staffs, piece by piece, skillfully (artfully) laid one design after another,

creating a collage display; an artwork of its own.

What's on Your Mind?

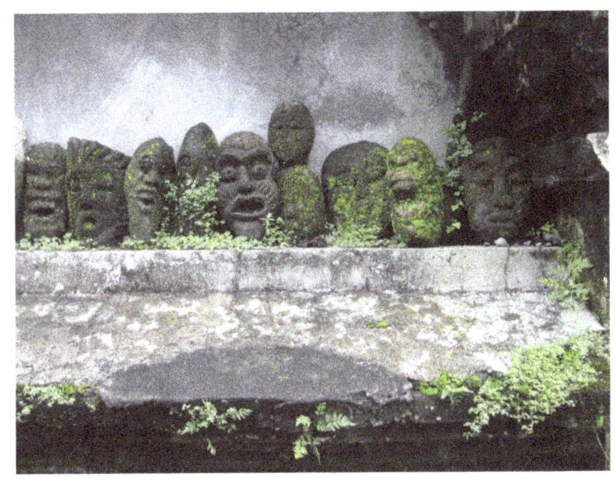

If all heads can talk
Curious what they must have thought
If all views aren't blocked

Photo taken in 2012

Location: Ubud, Indonesia

Another photographer nearby said, "I want to see what you see."

When One Paints the Sky

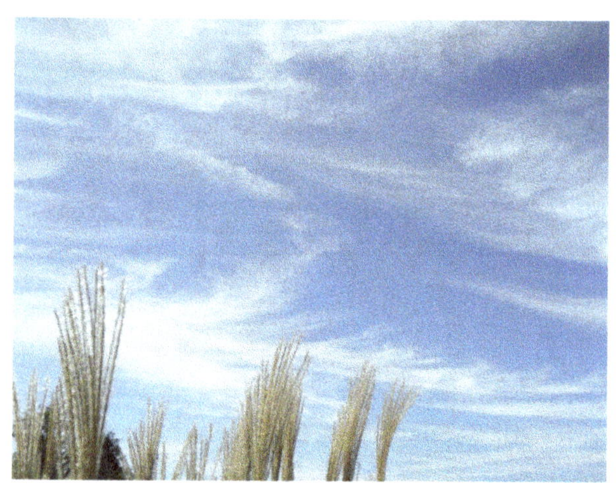

Their shapes talk and poke
In calligraphy brushstroke
Whispered as they spoke

Photo taken in 2020

Location: Utsunomiya, Japan

I was on a bike, looking for some plants to photo.

I stopped and squatted to get close to the ground,

but the sky was already painted,

and the brushes were there.

When the Sun is Low

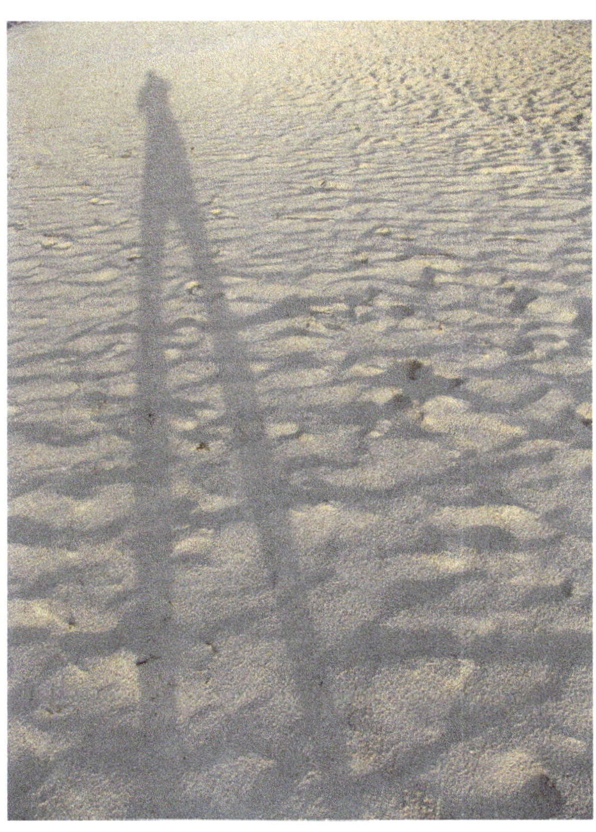

When the sun is low
And long stretches the shadow
The moon may still glow

Photo taken in 2011

Location: Somewhere in the Dominican Republic

Leaving my footprints behind as I followed my shadow, the wave-like pattern of the sand may be formed during high tide the night before, but it faithfully blankets the entire beach with light, shade, and shadows. As the sun goes higher, the shadows get shorter until it disappears.

Widow of the Wall

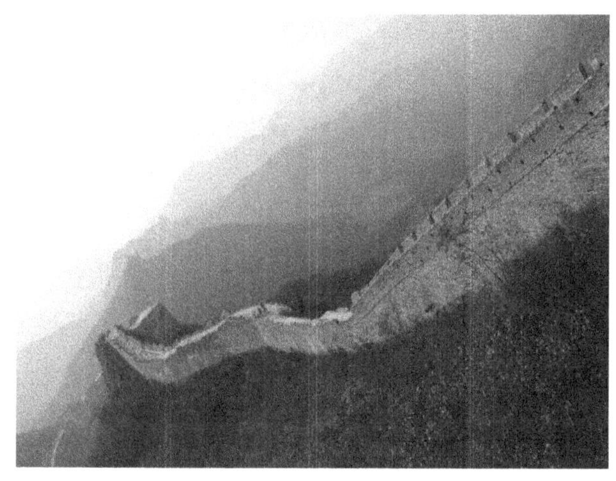

And she came alone
To where he toiled stone by stone
Entombed was his bone

Photo taken in 2018

Location: Simatai-Jinshanling Section, China

Took the bus, I was told to get off at a reservoir. From there I arranged a "taxi" to drop me off near the wall and pick me up in another location three or four hours later. That other location was based on the driver's estimated time to walk and climb (some steep sections required four limbs); and rest in between. With almost no one else in sight, it felt desolated, but serene.

More information about the legendary widow of the wall:

https://uwapress.uw.edu/book/9780295987842/meng-jiangnu-brings-down-the-great-wall/

Wrinkles

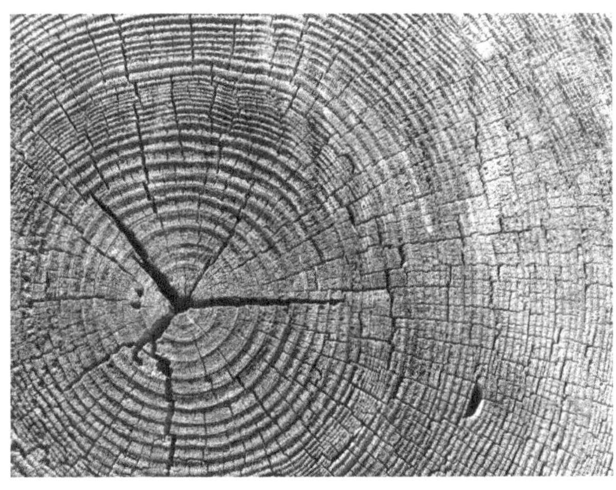

Droplets draw ripples
Rings and grooves carved in riddles
Wisdom in wrinkles

Photo taken in 2023

Location: Halifax, Canada

Ripples from droplets on water has the opposite pattern of the rings in tree trunks. One accelerates, the other decelerates; seen in the distances between their ridges and grooves. It takes longer for nutrients to reach the outer rings as the trunk ages, hence the growth is slower. This trunk is part of the promenade along the Halifax Waterfront Boardwalk.

Zigzag in an Alley

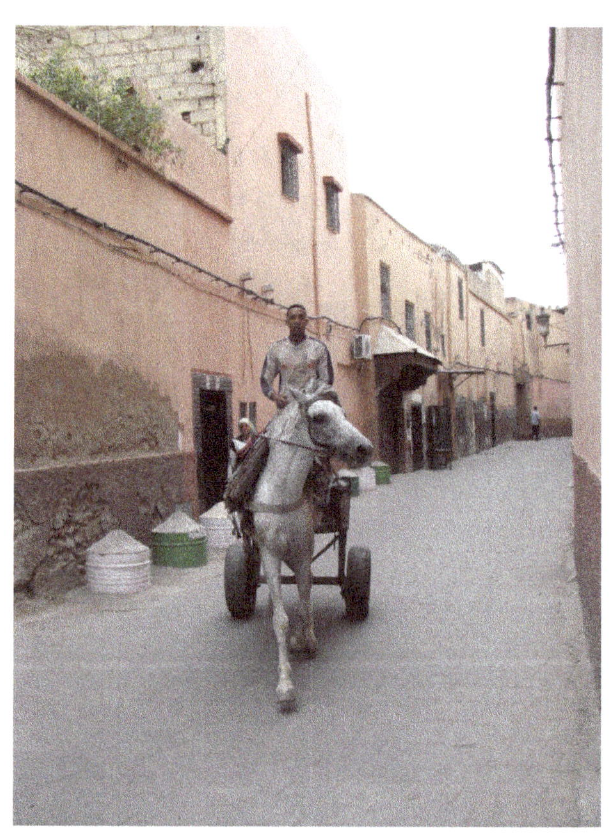

Zigzagging trotter
Hazard around the corner
One darts for cover

Photo taken in 2018

Location: Marrakech, Morocco

The beast was out of control.

The coachman shouted to no avail.

Everyone cleared the way.

Vincent Nugroho is a multifaceted individual, blending his passions for teaching, poetry, writing, and photography into an enchanting journey of exploration. Originally from Indonesia, Vincent has embraced diverse experiences, from teaching architectural history and interior design in Canada to embarking on adventures that span continents.

As an intrepid traveler, Vincent has roamed from the enchanting landscapes of Morocco, Turkey, and South Africa to the vibrant cultures of China, India, Japan, and Egypt. During his days as an architecture student, he embarked on a whirlwind journey through ten European countries in just ten days, armed with only a borrowed camera and boundless creativity. Vincent's inquisitive spirit and wanderlust have led him to various corners of the globe, where he has documented culture and vernacular architecture through his insightful articles.

Beyond his globetrotting endeavors, Vincent actively gives back to society through his volunteer work at Halifax Public Libraries, the Canadian Cancer Society, and the Nova Scotia Multicultural Festival. As a soccer coach at a local school and a street decorator in Bali, he invests his time and talents to uplift others.

Vincent's vibrant personality shines through his love for sweet treats, especially ice cream and chocolate. In his leisure moments, he plunges into a diverse array of non-fiction literature, particularly those that delve into travel and adventure. An avid musician, he finds joy in playing the guitar and saxophone, though he admits to being a terrible singer. Embracing a healthy lifestyle, Vincent practices yoga daily, and has triumphed over smoking, yet finds solace in a well-sweetened cup of coffee.

Living in Halifax, Canada, he relishes the simplicity of riding his bike and canoeing amidst the beauty of nature. Vincent's zest for life and dedication to personal growth is an inspiration to those around him, making him a cherished member of every community he touches.

For more information visit https://vincentnugroho.wixsite.com/online